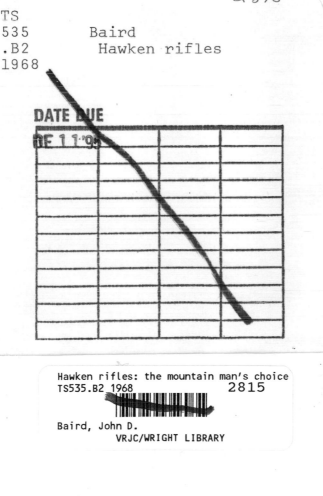

HAWKEN RIFLES

The Mountain Man's Choice

HAWKEN RIFLES

The Mountain Man's Choice

by

John D. Baird

ISBN 0-88227-010-9

© COPYRIGHT JOHN D. BAIRD 1968

SECOND PRINTING	1971
THIRD PRINTING	1972
FOURTH PRINTING	1973
FIFTH PRINTING	1974
SIXTH PRINTING	1976

THE BUCKSKIN PRESS

Big Timber, Mt. 59011

Reprint Edition Published by
THE GUN ROOM PRESS
127 Raritan Ave., Highland Park, N.J.
1976
By arrangement with the author

From an original oil painting by Judy Kelly, done as a special favor to an armchair "Mountain Man".

JOHN D. BAIRD

Table Of Contents

We dedicate this, the second printing of this volume, to all the Hawken enthusiasts about the country. They made this book possible, and it is to them that the author owes an undying debt of gratitude. Old Jake and Sam would have been proud of you.

jdb

Overleaf

JAMES E. SERVEN, noted author and collector, has graciously permitted the use of the two photographs found on the following pages. Mr. Serven's collection of seven Hawken rifles illustrates the typical broad buttstock, curved cheekpiece, and the integral set triggers and trigger guard. Distinctive is the heavy octagonal barrel, the double barrel keys, the simple sights and the plain iron trim that does not reflect light.

Note also that while each rifle is of a recognizable style, all have the individual characteristics found in hand-made rifles, and that none are exact duplicates of any of the others.

Close examination will reveal such points of variance as shape and construction of buttplate, the shape of lock and lock-section, style of comb, and contour of the snail of the patent-breech.

Other points of variance are the front and rear sights, and their placement, length of barrel, and its width, as measured across the flats, shape and material of forend tip, and the location and spacing of barrel key escutcheons.

Wood may be walnut, plain or striped maple, and both half-stocks and fullstocks were made in the Hawken epoch.

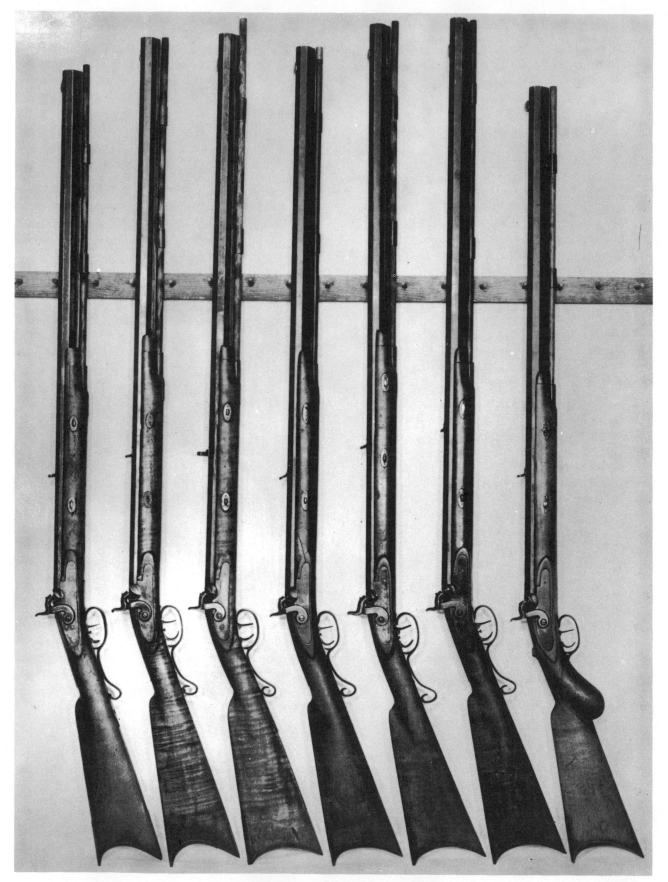

PLATE NO. 1 (described in overleaf)

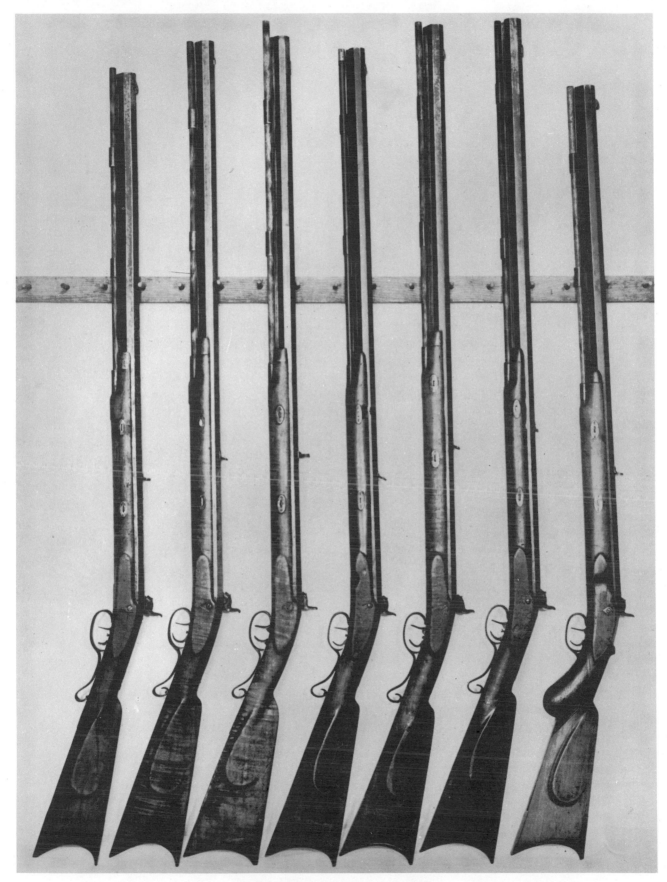

PLATE NO. 2   (described in overleaf)

After all the pictures were in, the galley proofs read, page proofs checked, the index made up, and a deep sigh of relief signifying that now, perhaps, we could go to press, one other point was gently brought to our attention. In one way or another, we managed to mention just about everyone we know, but we find that we have neglected one very important person.

It is with mingled feelings of pride and consternation that I mention my wife Vivian, who, between cooking, cleaning, and caring for two little boys and a big one, still found time to type and retype the manuscript for this volume.

We offer her our heartfelt gratitude for the many hours spent typing, listening to the author test his phrasing, and explaining to the neighbors why John D. was off looking at guns again. We hope that when she sees this, she will restore our broken dinner plate.

J.D.B.

Introduction

THE TREMENDOUS interest now being shown Hawken rifles is a direct result of published material by such writers as James Serven, Ned Roberts, John Barsotti, C. E. Hanson Jr. and many others. These men, and other writers like them, whose deep interest in Jacob and Samuel Hawken, and in the rifles these brothers produced in St. Louis during the period from 1807 to 1862, has provided the shooting fraternity with a wealth of information concerning Hawken rifles. However, such was not always the case, for when this writer first became interested in Hawken rifles, very little could be learned about them. It was only after diligent research could anything in print be found, and in this case, James Serven's article in MUZZLE BLASTS magazine, May 1945, was the first written work on Hawken discovered. This article was found after going through stacks of back issues of this magazine.

Since that time, this writer has been fortunate to have found many sources of information, some contradictory, but all very interesting, and all adding to his store of knowledge concerning a subject he has found fascinating for many years. As he pursued his quest for more information, he slowly became aware that he was not alone in his search, for each year he found others engaged in the same quest.

In his efforts to build a really accurate copy of a Hawken rifle, many attempts were made, but each attempt was hampered by the same difficulty. This was the lack of information on the details of a Hawken rifle. What did a Hawken really look like? How did it feel? What was that mysterious aura that made one rifle a Hawken, and another very nearly like it so plainly not a Hawken? Surely not just age, for we have among us rifle-makers who are capable of producing fine flint-lock full-stocked rifles that are spitting images of those carried by our grand-fathers throughout Pennsylvania, Ohio, Kentucky, and Tennessee when to travel here without a rifle was to invite the loss of hair. Books, pictures, and a good supply of original rifles make it fairly easy to duplicate the lines of an original Pennsylvania rifle, be it flint or cap-lock. But a Hawken, that's something else! How do you build a Hawken rifle from a picture in a magazine, or even from pictures taken of an original rifle in a museum some-place, were you lucky enough to know where such a place might be. It is easy to take measurements, pictures, pen-cil rubbings and so forth, but when you gather your wood and metal together to start construction, many, many little nagging questions start rearing their dirty little heads. Is this an exact template of the wrist, or of the forend, or of the cheek-piece? Was the light such, that when I took this picture, the line from the trigger guard to the forend tip appears to have just a suggestion of a belly in it? Was the comb full, or did it come to a sharp edge and just how did that front sight look? Can you remember all of these little details?

Probably you think that perhaps one or two deviations will not hurt the finished rifle, and after all, you don't wish to make a forgery of a famous rifle. When you finish the rifle, and proudly show your handiwork around, you slowly become aware that a deviation here and deviation there, plus little errors caused by lack of information have all combined to give you a heavy, big-bored, half-stocked rifle but definitely not a Hawken. Perhaps you have never been fortunate enough to handle a real Hawken, and you are happily unaware that you have not accomplished what you set out to do. This writer feels that if you, like himself, are enough of a Hawken fan to want a copy of a Hawken rifle, then you want as close a copy as it is humanly possible to get.

And why not a Hawken copy? One of Kit Carson's guns was a copy of a Hawken, made by B. J. Mills, of Harrodsburg, Kentucky, so it would seem that to a Mountain Man, or his modern-day armchair counterpart, a Haw-ken copy was and is better than no Hawken at all. Even if they were not scarce, and all who wished to own one could be gratified, it would still be folly to risk losing one through accident in the woods or on the range. So for those who would be Mountain Men, if they be real men, they are going to want a Hawken copy, and most are going to have to build their own. This is being done all over the country, as Bill Large of Ironton, Ohio, will attest. One of the best barrel makers in the business, he reports that he is nearly swamped with orders for Hawken type barrels.

The secret to building an accurate reproduction of a Hawken, aside from the maker's skill at work of this nature, lies in having full information on the particular rifle being duplicated. This information can be in the form of pictures, drawings, measurements, and pencil rubbings. Equally important to success is strict adherence to those measurements, with no deviations whatsoever. The very plainness of a Hawken rifle leads the eye to its basic lines, with no fancy fittings to mask those little errors here and there. The basic lines of the rifle must be correct or the rifle will never have that look or feel that is so a part of Hawken rifles.

One of the most misleading statements that appears so regularly in Hawken rifle descriptions goes something like this: Hawken rifles were short, heavy barreled, thick of wrist and wide of butt, with no grace, etc. etc. I would disagree most heartily with this description per se. Certainly Hawken rifles, particularly the later ones, were heavier and sturdier than the Pennsylvania rifle, but even so, they retained a grace and symmetry of form that is pleasing to the eye. The quality of workmanship of the Hawken shop steadily improved through the years, and the fittings and finish of a Hawken rifle needs no apology. To compare a Hawken rifle to a J. Henry or a Leman trade rifle would be equal to today's comparison between a fine custom built rifle and a cheap mail order gun.

The Hawken brothers took great pride in their rifles, and you can bet nothing went out of their shop that did not meet their approval. Sam Colt wanted Samuel Hawkens to be his St. Louis distributor for Colt products, but Sam would not, preferring to handle only what they, the Hawken shop, produced. These were sold at a modest price of $25.00 to $40.00 each, even though they were bringing much more on the frontier. Were the Hawken rifle anything but a fine, well built, dependable rifle, it would not have reached the pinnacle of esteem it held with such men as Bridger, Carson and others who depended upon their rifles for their very lives.

Hawken rifles were used by men who played a large part in the development of improvement in the rifle itself. A Missouri ridge-runner turned Rocky Mountain trapper had no qualms about telling a Yankee gun-tinkerer what he wanted when he brought in a rifle broken through the wrist from a fall from a horse, or one with the trigger guard torn away from a hand to hand scuffle with a redskin. If he wanted a bigger caliber rifle to kill that grizzly that had mauled him after being stung with a light rifle, you can bet Jake and Sam went to work to make him what he wanted. Improvements in the Hawken were rapid because each change was brought about to satisfy customer demands, and as proven sound in use, were incorporated into succeeding rifles as a matter of course.

Every war in recorded history has brought about rapid advancement in the development of new and improved weapons. This is a proven fact. This was a war of sorts; man against the wilderness, against bigger and tougher wild animals, and against a cruel and wiley foe, the horse mounted Indians of the Plains. The Hawken shop didn't just happen to build a rifle suited for the use it would receive in the West. The "Rocky Mountain Rifle" came into being through successive improvements in existing styles of rifles, and through these improvements, the Tennessee and Pennsylvania style rifle was transformed into a more compact, sturdier, harder hitting rifle, and in the transformation, completely lost its identification as such, and came to be known as a mountain rifle.

The writer can think of no single feature of a Hawken rifle that has come down through the plus-40 years of Hawken rifle production, unchanged from the first rifle to the last rifle made by Sam. Be it buttplate, trigger or guard, barrel, stock, sights, breech, tang, cheekpiece, or what have you. All details of the rifle underwent changes and improvements, and the only thing that this writer can think of that has not been appreciably changed has been the ramrod guides and lower thinble. These parts were more nearly alike on all Hawken rifles examined than any other feature, and because of this, offer absolutely no help in determining the date of manufacture of any particular rifle.

It is these very changes and improvements that help one make some reasonable, accurate deductions concerning any particular rifle. Dating a Hawken is guess work at best, since none were dated as to manufacture, but it is possible to come acceptably close by utilizing knowledge of various epochs of rifle building. For instance, Roberts, in his book, *"The Muzzle-loading Caplock Rifle,"* states that while the patent breech was invented as early as 1787, he implies that it did not come into common use until about 1840. It can be assumed that Jake and Sam kept abreast of all new developments in the riflemaking business, and were quick to adopt any improvement that would help them hold their lead in the gun trade. The dates 1822 to 1849 also give us a definite period in which to place all guns marked J. & S. Hawken, for these dates include that period of time that the partnership between Jake and Sam was in effect. After Jake's death from cholera in 1849, Sam continued the business alone, stamping his rifles S. Hawken, St. Louis.

At the risk of seeming to be somewhat of a fanatic on this point, this writer wants to emphasize that the Hawken rifle was not a huge, clumsy, heavy club of a gun, as some descriptions would lead you to believe. To describe a Hawken as a 12 or 15 pound rifle, firing a half ounce ball ahead of huge quantities of powder is a little like saying that all horses have big feet and pull beer wagons. Certainly some Hawken rifles did weight as much as 12 pounds, and some even weighed as much as 15 pounds, but these rifles were the exception, rather than the rule. These rifles were made up on special order, for and as very special purpose guns, for customers who wished the ultimate in long range accuracy and shocking power. Double charging a rifle does increase the range somewhat, but it does so at the expense of accuracy. Double charging was resorted to, more to increase velocity, and thereby increasing energy, for close range targets, such as bear, and perhaps Indians.

To effectively increase range in a round ball rifle, you must increase ball weight, or size. A .64 or .68 caliber rifle will shoot farther than a .50 caliber rifle, simply because the heavier ball will retain its velocity for a longer period, and being heavier, will strike harder at long range. The winds will play havoc with a light ball but the heavier ball will drift less, making shots under difficult situations possible. Such features would be most desirable to a hide-hunter shooting buffalo from a stand, or a sea-otter hunter shooting from the beach. The Hawken rifles carried by the early trappers were not generally this large of bore, simply because you could not conveniently carry enough ammunition on your person to make such a rifle practical for an extended hunt.

It should also be understood that just because Horace Kephart tested his Hawken rifle with various charges, among them 164 and 203 grains of 2ff deadshot, it does not mean that the Mountain Man consistently charged his rifle with this much powder. It was meant to show the Hawken rifle was strong enough to stand this double charging, and that such a charge could be fired off the shoulder without too much shaking up. A bit of thinking will convince most of us that with powder selling for a dollar a pint, and the nearest source of supply over a thousand miles away, the Mountain Man, whether he carried a Hawken, a J. Henry, a Golcher, or even a Hudson Bay fusil, charged his piece with just enough powder to give acceptable accuracy and range. In the case of a .50 or .53 caliber Hawken, this would lie between 80 and 120 grains of powder ,depending upon the individual rifle, and its owner's ideas of acceptable accuracy and range. Kephart, himself, stated that he got the best accuracy from his Hawken with 82 grains of 2ff deadshot powder.

Most Hawken rifles weighed in the neighborhood of 10½ pounds, be it fullstocked, or halfstocked. The halfstock's rib and thimbles does not appreciably reduce the weight of the rifle, but it does render this part of the rifle less liable to breakage. Something very important when you are many months from the nearest source of repair.

This may be a good place to point out that a pound of lead will produce about 32 .53 caliber balls or approximately 40 of the .50 caliber balls. A large horn, of the type carried by the Mountain Man, would hold about a pound and a half of powder. With an average charge of 100 grains of powder per shot, and even allowing generously for lead recovery, it still would be necessary for the hunter to carry at least a hundred balls to properly utilize his powder. Ammunition would, of course, also be carried upon the pack animals, but we speak here of what he would carry on his person. There would be no need to carry more balls than he had powder to fire, nor would he carry more powder than needed to furnish a charge for these balls he was able to carry in his pouch.

Here seems to be the crux of the matter. The need for an ample supply of ammunition, balanced by the need for bullet weight and heavy charges, and its attendant weight problem, led to a compromise. The early .50 caliber Hawken fit this compromise most admirably, and it was later, as supply problems diminished, and ranges became somewhat extended, that the .53 caliber and heavier bores came into the forefront.

This writer has been an enthusiastic miner in the Hawken Lode for many years, but each nugget of information was uncovered at the expense of much digging and probing of old magazines, bookstores, and libraries. Often one bit of information would lead to another, and correspondence with other Hawken enthusiasts opened new avenues of exploration. The growing flood of interest in Hawken rifles being shown by the members of the National Muzzle Loading Rifle Association came as no surprise to him. He had felt this interest and has watched it grow for the past few years. With his own experiences at trying to build a good Hawken copy with inadequate information on the detail of an original Hawken, he has hopefully waited for one of the better known authors to write a book that would fulfill the needs of this fast growing group of Hawken buffs. When no such volume was forthcoming, he resolved to write such a book himself. As a first step in this direction, he contacted the editor of *Muzzle Blasts* magazine, the monthly organ of the National Muzzle Loading Rifle Association, to see if they were interested in a series of articles on the Hawken rifle. The enthusiasm with which his proposal was received greatly strengthened his resolve to write a book on the subject. It is impossible at this time to include material on every known existing Hawken, but every effort has been made to give a good representative cross section of Hawken rifle production. Special emphasis has been placed on those points of special interest to the muzzle-loading rifle student and builder.

Drawing upon his own experiences in shooting this type of weapon, building them, and studying the history of the times and the people contemporary to Hawken rifles, this author has made his own deductions where deductions were necessary to bridge a gap in information. He has made assumptions where it seemed assumptions could be safely made, and he has relied heavily on such authorities as Horace Kephart and James Serven. After years of reading and digesting Hawken lore, it is somewhat difficult to separate what is original thinking and what is merely the result of much reading of the published work of others. Therefore, when any particularly well put phrase rolls out of my fingers and into print, it is not a deliberate pirating of words, but an unconscious tribute to some other writer who said it better, first.

The pictures, for the most part, are those taken by the author, as he became able to travel to distant parts in order to personally examine those rifles described herein. As anyone of limited means is fully aware, travel is hard to justify, and easy to put off, when the family budget is involved. A number of years transpired between the first pictures acquired, and the last ones garnered for this book.

As has been stated before, the reason for this book's very being is to furnish an aid to those who would build a Hawken copy. The material was gathered and presented in this particular way for that purpose. The written material is presented with the hope that it will help in the more full understanding of Hawken, as well as giving a little background as to the original owner of the rifle, wherever that has been possible. In most cases, nothing was known of the rifle's history, and a great deal of conjecture can be resorted to. Perhaps it is the author's complete addiction to Hawken rifles that creates the mood, but it is easy, when cradling one of these rifles in your arms, to find yourself riding with Carson, or Bridger, or sitting in front of a campfire with Modena, Meek, Williams, Tobin, and a host of others. It is sincerely hoped that this volume will enable others to enjoy such dreams, and help them to build a rifle, that like LaBonte's, really makes 'em come!

Preface

To FULLY understand and appreciate the Hawken "Rocky Mountain Rifle," one must associate it with that era of history in which it gained prominence. The study of history comes in many forms, and one of the most pleasant of these is the reading of those engaging little receptacles of human knowledge called books. We are indebted to those few writers who ventured into the early West, so that they might have first hand knowledge of life on the prairies and in the mountains, and who wrote knowingly and well of their experiences. Those few have made it possible for present generations to have an understanding of the events that preceded and attended the era that gave us the "Mountain Man".

When first contemplating this volume, we did not visualize anything other than a well illustrated text on Hawken rifles. Subsequent thinking has led us to the point where we feel it is equally as important to discuss the men who made these rifles, some of the men who used them, and also to include a few words concerning those intrepid men of letters who came, who saw, and whose books and paintings left future generations their only contact with those turbulent times.

Concerning noted artists like Catlin, Remington, Russell, and Bierstadt, there is nothing we can say that would add one whit to the silent testimonial given by the paintings alone. To see such paintings, as are in the Gilcrease Institute, for instance, is an awe inspiring experience—words do not suffice. To see is to love—surely something more than just the hand of man was at work, to bring us so close to reality, through paint and brush.

A record of life on the prairie as told by Francis Parkman in his book *"Oregon Trail,"* offers one of the best insights available to us of the atmosphere and character of the Plains. Although containing literary mannerisms that are considered old fashioned today, it brings to life the West as it was before the multitude of people destroyed the very charm that had drawn them. Parkman's visit, coming as it did in 1846, coincided with important events in the ever evolving West. The legionary rendezvous of the fur brigades were a thing of the past, but there were still plenty of Mountain Men in the country. The Indian tribes were comparatively quiet, it being the lull before the storms, so to speak. The huge numbers of emigrant trains, the destruction of the buffalo herds, the resultant Indian wars were yet to come. In 1846, only a few hardy souls were braving the wilderness to travel to Oregon, the Indian looked upon the whites as the source of goods he had come to depend on, the buffalo herds were intact, and while the price for beaver was undeniably low, there were many who were certain it could not remain at this ridiculously low price, and was bound to rise. Trappers were hanging on in the mountains, with this hope; their only hope really, since many had no desire to go anywhere else, or do anything but continue the way of life they had been enjoying.

Fresh in the minds of these trappers were the stories of those early days of exploration of virgin territories, in the search for beaver; the dangers, death, and rewards that had been theirs. Embellished by many tellings around evening camp, or long days in winter lodges, it made fascinating listening to the young, impressionable visitor from the East. Parkman's early desire to make his life's work the writing of history prompted his trip West to study first hand the remaining "wild" Indians and their village life. He could not have been anything but a rapt audience, while first hand accounts of battle with Indians, danger and death, love, anger, or riches came from all sides. Tinged with the superstitions and folklore of the times, spiced with outright lies quite often, nevertheless, a group of Mountain Men swapping stories around a fire invariably held their audience of green horns spellbound.

Although Parkman was plagued by ill health most of his adult life, in his youth he was a great believer in rigorous sports and exercise, and as a result, was quite fit. He, even as a young man, was one of scholarly reserve, but it is significant to note that he was fond of wandering in the woods at home with his rifle as his sole companion. He was reputed to be a skilled marksman with this rifle, which he had dubbed "Satan". Fresh out of Harvard, with the physical fitness and enthusiasm of his youth, he was to take to the life on the prairies with a verve and spontaneity that was to win him acceptance among those Mountain Men he came into contact with.

In preparation for his trip to the West, Parkman had visited with the fur trader Nathaniel Wyeth, lately returned to Massachusetts. He also visited St. Louis in the spring of 1845, a year after his graduation from Harvard. It was at this preliminary trip to St. Louis that arrangements were initiated towards obtaining a guide, and equipment for the trip, to be made the following year. One can imagine the excitement with which he walked the streets of St. Louis, visiting with Fitzpatrick and Pierre Chouteau, watching as workmen graded and bundled packets of furs that had come down river, relishing the odors of fur, leather, guns, traps, harness, sweat, and all the odors of a huge warehouse that had been the focal point of the fur trade in St. Louis since founding of the city.

With the river front landings lined with steamboats, and the hustle and bustle of loading and unloading of cargoes, the piercing whistle of escaping steam, the laughter and song of drunken boat men, loungers, Mountain Men, traders, Indians, gamblers, and all the others who went to make up this hodge-podge crossroads of nations, would serve as a powerful stimulant to this young man's enthusiasm. No doubt he made it a point to seek out those who had been to the mountains, and questioned all who would give him answers.

With the information garnered from these sources, and from counseling of such men as Fitzpatrick and Chouteau, he would have arrived at some intelligent conclusions as to what was needed in the way of arms for the proposed trip. He, no doubt, spent many long hours in the gunshops of Hawken, Hoffman & Campbell, and others, who were making and selling guns for the Western trade. It is on this first trip that he placed an order for a St. Louis made rifle to be delivered to him upon his return to St. Louis the following spring.

On April 13, 1846, Parkman returned to St. Louis, traveling by riverboat, and took rooms at the Planters Hotel. He was soon joined by his traveling companion, Quincy A. Shaw, and the two set about concluding final arrangements for the trip.

During the preceding winter, the Chouteaus had arranged for a guide for the two, acquiring the services of one Henry Chatillon, with whom Parkman became great friends. In addition, Parkman was given a letter of introduction by John Clapp, agent for the Chouteaus, guaranteeing him welcome and succor at any of the company's posts.

Parkman equipped himself with a pair of pistols, and took delivery of his "long, heavy rifle," as he described it, for which he exchanged a good smooth-bore gun and ten dollars. A detailed description of this rifle is found in Chapter Seven. That he was acting on the advice of experienced counselors is apparent, since he left his rifle "Satan" back East, knowing that it was unsuitable for western use. His papers reveal that he paid $14.00 for the pair of pistols; apparently used, since they also include a notation of $1.00 for pistol repair.

Parkman spent the summer of 1846 on the plains, and lived for some time among the Indians. The incidents and adventures of his trip were published in book form as the "Oregon Trail." Upon his return from the mountains, he presented his rifle to his guide, Henry Chatillon, as Chatillion's rifle had seen better days, and as Parkman says, "It was an excellent piece, which he (Chatillion) was always fond of using."

After his trip with Parkman, Chatillion made only two more trips to the mountains. He returned to the employment of the American Fur Company as a hunter. On May 15, 1847, he left St. Louis on the steamboat "Martha" for Fort Union. The ship's log, kept by a clerk named Finch, contains many accounts of his hunting and the game he brought in. Again in 1854, he and his brother went West as guides for Sir George Gore, a wealthy Irishman who took with him 40 servants, 112 horses, 12 yoke of oxen, 6 wagons, and 21 carts loaded with every conceivable luxury and necessity.

On October 5, 1858, he was married to Mrs. Odile Delor, widow of John Lux. Odile Delor Lux was his cousin, and also a woman of considerable property. Thereafter Chatillion was almost entirely concerned with the real estate business in St. Louis. He and his wife had no children. Henry Chatillion died August 7, 1873, in St. Louis, and was buried in the Mount Olive Catholic Cemetery.

Chatillion's St. Louis wife evidently was not pleased by his association with the Indians. Only recently in the old Chatillion home, hidden under the attic eaves, was found a rolled up portrait, cracked and dark with age, of an Indian woman and child. It is believed to be his Indian wife "Bear Robe" whose death is recorded by Parkman in the "Oregon Trail".

Parkman visited Chatillion in St. Louis in 1869, and the visit is mentioned in his writing. The visit is also mentioned in a letter by Parkman to his sister Eliza, dated August 1, 1869. Chatillion enjoyed a brief period of notoriety as a celebrity, when Parkman's book was published, but later sank back into obscurity, and up on his death, was virtually unknown.

The year following Parkman's visit to the western prairies, came another young man, with the ability to record in interesting fashion, what he saw and heard while visiting the west. George Frederic Ruxton, a young Englishman, who came to the mountains by way of Mexico, seeking excitement and adventure, and finding it in the company of the mountain men, wrote of his adventures for Blackwood's *"Edinburgh Magazine"*. The stories ran serially in those publications of 1848. Told for the most part in the vernacular of the mountain men, Ruxton's writing gives us one of our most graphic records of life in the mountains, and upon the prairies.

Condensed into book form, under the title *"Life In The Far West,"* this volume is required reading for anyone interested in learning more about early western history. Published by the University of Oklahoma Press, edited by LeRoy R. Hafen, it is one of several good books brought out concerning the period that we are interested in. Ruxton's uncanny ability to write in the vernacular of the prairie, without the tendency of contemporary writers to romanticize unreasonably, gives this generation one of its few peeps at mountain life as it really was.

About the turn of the century, because of greatly expanding interest in the west, and the mystery and excitement attached to its unknown expanses, unknown that is, by the majority of the eastern population, it is easy to understand the popularity with which any written word of life on the prairie and in the mountains was received by the general public. Those few of the mountain travelers who were literate enough, often made some attempt to write up their memoirs, or were encouraged to tell their stories to enterprising writers of the times. Quite often the stories are exaggerated in the telling, either from the desire for notoriety by the teller, or from dressing up by the writer, in his romantic, but questionable, efforts to make better reading. It is quite often we have to read such accounts with a grain of salt, keeping in mind that we are searching for information, not serving as a literary critic.

"My Sixty Years on the Plains" by Bill Hamilton is an example. If one took the book literally, he could only reach the conclusion that Hamilton was solely responsible for all the great things that happened in the West; that there was nothing impossible for him to accomplish, and that if he had not gone West, very likely it would still be in the hands of the Indians. Quite aside from this aspect of the literary effort, it must be recognized as a very useful source of information concerning life on the prairie during those early days. Hamilton's acquaintance with other noted mountain men, his knowledge of places, events, and arms all furnish us with a mass of knowledge concerning this interesting subject. If we judge the book on this basis, it becomes most worthwhile, and should be a part of the library of the student of western history.

While we feel no necessity for us to list all the books we feel are pertinent to this subject, we do feel that we would be derelict in our duty, or something, if we did not mention two other books of note.

We speak of *"Wah-to-Yah, And The Taos Trail"* by Garrard, and *"Across The Wide Missouri"* by Bernard DeVoto. There are countless books that are most interesting, but these two are simply chucked full of information for the armchair mountain man. We heartily recommend that they find a place on the reader's shelf of fine books.

Saint Louis 25 April 1846

To any person or persons in our
employ in the Indian Country

This will be presented by our friends Mr. F. Parkman and Mr. Quincy A. Shaw, who visit the interior of the country for their pleasure and amusement, and whom we beg to recommend to your kind & friendly attentions.

If the gentlemen shall be in need of anything in the way of supplies, etc. you will oblige us by furnishing them to the extent of their wants, as also to render them any & every aid in your power, of which they may stand in need.

Very truly yours,
P. Chouteau Jr. & Co.
John Clapp

Signature of Mr. F. Parkman
do   Quincy A. Shaw

The above is a copy of the handwritten letter of introduction given Francis Parkman, by John Clapp, who, as agent for the Chouteaus, handled the arrangements for Parkman's tour of the West.

Chronological Record Of Events Connected With Hawken Shop

1807   Jacob Hawken first arrives in St. Louis

1813   Joshua Shaw develops percussion cap

1814   Shaw attempts to patent his invention

1815   Jacob Hawken opens gunshop in St. Louis

1821   Jacob Hawken is listed at 214 N. Main St., St. Louis

1822   Samuel Hawken comes to St. Louis from Xenia, Ohio

1826   Item on Hawken bill to Indian Dept., May 9th, $.50 for shoeing horse

1835   Samuel made pistol for son William (cost $12.00)

1836   St. Louis directory lists S. Hawken at 21 Laurel (no mention of J&S Hawken)

1842   Christian Hoffman & Tristam Campbell—working as gunsmiths for Hawken

1845   Christian Hoffman

Christopher M. Hawken (son of Jacob Hawken)

Tristam Campbell—listed as Hoffman & Campbell, 65 Locust

J&S Hawken factory listed at 33 Washington Ave.

S. Hawken listed at 37 Washington Ave.

(Note—Laurel St. has its name changed to Washington by city ordinance between 1842 and 1845.)

1847-48   Christian Hoffman

Christopher Hawken

Tristam Campbell—listed as Hoffman & Campbell, 65 Locust

1849   Hoffman & Campbell listed at 65 Locust

Jacob Hawken dies in cholera epidemic-believed to have been cremated with other cholera victims in frenzied efforts to halt the disease

Christopher Hawken goes West in search of gold

1850   Sam Hawken is listed alone

1854   Sam Hawken

William S. Hawken

Tristam Campbell—listed as Hawken & Campbell, 37 Washington

Christopher Hawken

Christian Hoffman—operating livery business, 13 & 14 Market

1857   Chistopher M. Hawken marries Mary Ann Eads, daughter of Granville Eads, and builds home (still standing) at 9442 West Big Ben Blvd.

1858   Samuel Hawken prepares to turn shop over to Wm. S. Hawken

1859   Wm. S. Hawken listed at 21 Washington Ave.

Samuel Hawken departs St. Louis, Apr. 20. 20-arrived Denver, Jun 30

Tristam Campbell listed as gunsmith at 76 Locust St.

1860   Wm. S. Hawkens sells Hawken shop to Wm. L. Watt & others

Wm. S. Hawken goes to Denver, Col.

William L. Watt listed at 21 Washington, advertising as successor to W. S. Hawken

Samuel Hawken opens gun shop in Denver, Jan.

1861   Samuel Hawken returns to St. Louis, in retirement

Wm. S. Hawken takes over Denver shop (Auraria)

1838   J. P. Gemmer is born (June) in Nassau, Germany

1855   Gemmer comes to America with his father (Booneville, Mo.)

1859   Gemmer finds employment with E. Kleinhenn, St. Louis

1860   Gemmer goes into employ of Wm. L. Watt, 21 Wash.

1861   Gemmer enlisted as gunsmith in Gov. Arsenal (Corporal)

1862   Gemmer buys share of Hawken business

1864   Edward's St. Louis directory lists Wm. L. Watt at 21 Wash.

1866   Gemmer is listed as proprietor at 21 Wash.

1874   Gemmer moves to 600 North Third Street

1876   Gemmer moves to 764 North Third Street

1880   Gemmer moves to 700 North Eight Street

1884   Samuel Hawken dies (May 9) at the home of his daughter and is buried in Bellefontaine Cemetery, St. Louis

1915   Gemmer closes down business and enters retirement

1919   Gemmer dies (Oct.) and is buried in Bellefontaine Cem.

CHAPTER 1

The Hawken Customer

THE AMERICAN fur trade was the culmination of a trade that had its origin in Europe, and had been going on for some four hundred years. Since about the middle of the 15th Century, a good beaver hat was part of the dress of the wealthy, considered a status symbol, and demanded by custom. Due to the peculiar quality of the barbed hair, which could be torn from the pelt and worked into a superior felt, the beaver's fur was in great demand by an ever increasing hatter's market. The abundance of beaver in the newly discovered North American continent played an important role in the events to take place in this new country. Exploration, colonization, trading posts and expeditions, treaties and alliances with the Indian tribes; all had their basis in the search for beaver, and the profits derived from such enterprise. Competition for beaver led to direct conflicts between governments, led to the degradation of Indian tribes, and nearly led to the extinction of beaver in this country.

The Lewis and Clark expedition of 1804 had returned with glowing accounts of the beaver and other fur bearing animals in the great new country they had traversed. French traders had been operating out of St. Louis and other villages up and down the river for many years, mainly with the Indians on the lower reaches of the Missouri River. Manual Lisa and the Chouteaus were among the first to send expeditions to the Indians of the Upper Missouri, to trade and trap for beaver. Hudson Bay men from Canada were reaching for this comparatively untapped source of furs, with posts in the Oregon country, and expeditions trading and trapping as far south and east as the Mandan villages.

Their attention and imagination kindled by this growing trade in the far West, two men, William H. Ashley and Andrew Henry, set into motion a plan that was to revolutionize the fur trading industry, and was to introduce a new breed of cat to the mountains. The St. Louis papers of 1822 carried the following advertisement.

TO ENTERPRISING YOUNG MEN

The subscriber wishes to engage ONE HUN-DRED MEN, to ascend the river Missouri to its source, there to be employed for one, two or three years—For particulars, enquire of Major Andrew Henry, near the Lead Mines, in the County of Washington, (who will ascend with, and command the party) or to the subscriber at St. Louis.

Wm. H. Ashley

In his effort to reduce overhead, Ashley did not hire these men at a fixed wage. Instead, he made arrangements with them to the effect that they would receive half of all furs collected, in exchange for supplies and transportation to the mountains. Once established in the mountains, Ashley was to take the furs collected by these free trappers, in exchange for supplies and cash, as needed by the trapper, at rates of exchange dictated by supply and demand. Previously to this innovation, all trappers had been hired as engagees by the organizers of such expeditions, and to institute such arrangements as Ashley's was to cause consternation among organized companies doing business the old way.

These first free trappers, or Ashley men, as they were called, felt they were far above the lowly engagee; being in business for themselves so to speak, and took great pride in their independence and freedom of action. Far from the restraints of civilization, the Mountain Men, as they called themselves, developed a culture of their own. Trapping for beaver in Spring and Fall, wintering in the mountains and coming in to the annual summer rendezvous, when caravans of trade goods came up from the States, the Mountain Man adapted to a new way of life. He adopted those Indian customs that served his purpose, lived off the bounty of the land in good times, starved in the bad times, and rejoiced in the freedom of mountain life. Many of the trappers had friends among the Indian tribes, and took Indian wives when it suited them. Such actions were encouraged by the traders, for it opened up new sources of business, both among the tribes, and with the trappers themselves, who now had need for "foo-fa-raw" for their new dependents.

Samuel Hawken's arrival in St. Louis in 1822

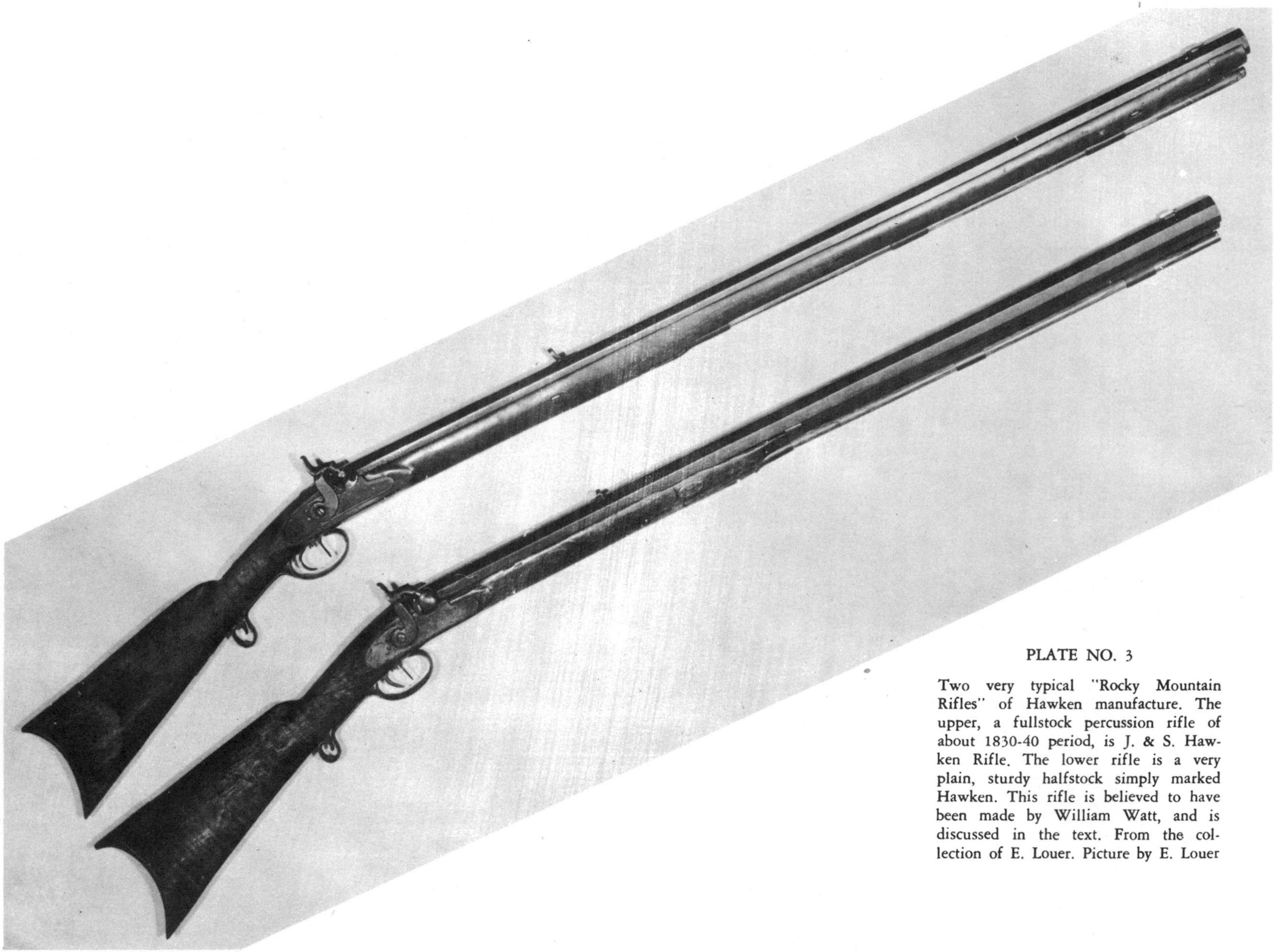

PLATE NO. 3

Two very typical "Rocky Mountain Rifles" of Hawken manufacture. The upper, a fullstock percussion rifle of about 1830-40 period, is J. & S. Hawken Rifle. The lower rifle is a very plain, sturdy halfstock simply marked Hawken. This rifle is believed to have been made by William Watt, and is discussed in the text. From the collection of E. Louer. Picture by E. Louer

2

PLATE NO. 4

The breech section of a late S. Hawken marked rifle. Note "Slant breech" feature, and that the lock bolt head is recessed into lock bolt escutcheon.

3

PLATE NO. 5

S. Hawken stamp on 1855-65 period rifle. The rear sight on these late Hawken rifles were often castings.

coincided with the greatly expanded push to harvest the furs in the far West. The trappers and traders were in great need of rifles, that could be depended upon for accuracy, sturdiness, and freedom from need of repair. The shop of Jacob and Samuel Hawken was ideally placed to receive a great share of this new business, and the rifles they made for this specialized trade were to become known as the "Hawken Rocky Mountain Rifle."

In the 1840's, the fashion in hats changed from beaver to those made of silk, and the great demand for beaver fur dropped dramatically. (Some students of this era maintain that it was the changing economy of European markets, as well as increased costs of transportation of furs gathered at far-flung points in our own west, that cut the price paid for furs in the mountains.) No longer was it profitable to send trading caravans to the mountains to supply the mountain men, and they were forced to come in to the various trading posts that had been built throughout the west. The last renrezvous was held in 1839, on the Green River, and it was announced that no more caravans would be sent to the mountains.

Jim Bridger, who had left St. Louis as an Ashley man in 1822, made his first return trip to that city, after an absence of seventeen years. Other mountain men scattered over the country, many with no desire to return to the settlements, and no means of supporting themselves in the mountains. A few organized horse stealing raids into the ranches of southern California and Mexico. Others served as guides and hunters for the growing

number of travelers upon the plains and through the mountains. Still others fell in with their wive's families, and lived with the Indians. A few went to California, and into the Wilimette Valley of Oregon, and made homes and farms there. The wild, boisterous days of the Mountain Man were coming to a close. Trappers, hunters, and adventurers would continue to roam the mountains, and continue to seek the pitifully few remaining beaver, but the era of organized expeditions as visualized by Henry and Ashley had ended.

The "Rocky Mountain Rifle" from the shop of Jacob and Samuel Hawken reached the pinnacle of esteem in the hearts of these mountain men because it combined sturdiness, simplicity and dependability with accuracy and great power. It was designed for a special purpose, and was carried and used by men who had no equal in the history of this country.

A thousand miles or more from any source of supply, in an uncharted wilderness of immense prairies, towering mountain ranges, rushing rivers and yawning chasms, the seekers after beaver pelts plied their dangerous trade. When possible, they lived with the Indians, and when this was undesirable, or impossible, went in large parties that could defy the red man, or in small parties that depended upon stealth and cunning to avoid and outwit their savage foe. Even though they were beset with danger from every hand, the beaver trappers worked the mountain streams with such skill and singleness of purpose that they nearly exterminated the beaver as a species. The silk hat is credited with ruining the fur trade, but in so doing, it preserved the

4

beaver from being completely trapped out of the mountain streams.

This breed of men, who daily risked their lives, while wrestling their living from the land, and riches from the streams, were a breed apart. Coming as they did, from every station in life, and out of the reach of so-called civilization and restraints, they developed an order and way of life that has known no equal either before their time or since. With survival depending upon skill and self-reliance, and death a quick reward for carelessness or stupidity, the mountain man who lived to die a quiet death in the settlements was a very unique personification of a multitude of skills.

A great many trappers lost their lives, and often their scalps, in the mountains. Usually from encounters with Indians, sometimes from quarrels among themselves, or from tangling with a grizzly, or even from being thrown from their horse, while running buffalo. Some met death from the elements, that was no less a foe than the most fierce of Indian tribes. Sudden blizzards, floods, dust storms, intense cold, or heat, with water holes turned to lakes of hardening mud-all were hazards to be met and overcome. It took a brave man, and a resourceful one, to ride into the unknown, and return months, or years later, with pack horses loaded with beaver, scalps at his belt, and a look in his eye that bespoke of far places and unimaginable terrors. Not always was the return so triumphant; all too often the trapper is reported crawling into some friendly camp, near death from wounds and exposure. After being waylaid and set upon by Indians, or embraced by an unfriendly grizzly, it was common for the victim, or rather his scattered bones, to be found in some lonely canyon by next year's trapping parties.

We do not intend to go into a long dialog about the Mountain Man. Much has been written, and the stories told in much more interesting fashion than could be told here. Carson, Bridger, Tobin, Meek, Fitzpatrick; all have their place in history, and have had their stories told repeatedly.

However, there is one element in these stories that is sadly lacking. Hardly any mention is made of the firearms used by these men, and rare indeed is a detailed description of any particular rifle. We are primarily interested in Hawken rifles, so it may be worth a bit of space to discuss those men whom it is known owned and used rifles from the shop of Jacob and Samuel Hawken.

First let us remind the reader that the single-shot, muzzle-loading rifle had its limitations. No matter how powerful, or accurate, or dependable, it still offered only one shot, and the user's skill determined how quickly he could reload and shoot again. Circumstances altered conditions, and regardless of how quick the rifleman could spit a ball down the barrel, it hardly ever

was fast enough. A fast firing, breech-loading rifle, or even faster repeating rifle, although of less power than a Hawken, would still offer tremendous advantages to the trapper facing an encircling horde of mounted Indians. Most of the mountain men who survived the life in the mountains long enough to see the advent of breech-loading arms, were quick to see their advantages, and adopted them post haste.

Bill Hamilton, in *"My Sixty Years On The Plains,"* tells us that his party exchanged their Hawken rifles for the new Sharps breech-loading rifles, at the same time acquiring a generous supply of the new paper cartridges for this arm.

Kit Carson has been credited with using a number of different guns, other than those from the shop of Hawken. Colt revolving pistols and rifles were among those mentioned as being carried by Carson. Fremont, for whom Carson served as guide, reported that he (Carson) carried two Paterson revolvers and a Colt revolving rifle on the expedition of 1842.

Bridger, who wore out a number of Hawken rifles, also carried for a time, a swivel barrel over and under rifle made by John Schuler, of Liverpool, Pennsylvania, so it would appear that all the mountain men were well aware of the need for more firepower than that afforded by a single shot muzzle-loader.

Livereating Johnson killed an Indian boy to get a Spencer rifle that had been rebuilt in the Hawken shop. Perhaps he thought that it might somehow give performance equal to the Hawken percussion rifle, but with the rapidity of fire inherent in the Spencer action. Since the breech-loader could only be as powerful as the cartridge designed to be fired in it, such conversions could hardly out-perform the regular Spencer rifles.

We have spoken elsewhere of Mariana Modena. Not much is known of his firearms, other than that he owned several Hawken rifles. The favorite of these is preserved in the Colorado Historical Museum, in Denver. This rifle is pictured and described in Chapter 6 of this volume.

Modena's rifle has an iron plate let into the bottom of the forend, presumably to serve as a wear plate against constant rubbing of the saddle, as it was carried in front of the rider. Jim Baker also had a Hawken so equipped, but these two are the only Hawken rifles to have such a feature that have come to this writer's attention. Possibly such a wear plate did not meet expectations, since the major portion of such wear fell on the sides of the forearm, rather than on the bottom. Forming and fitting such a plate would involve more expense, and was really not worth the extra trouble and cost.

The Bridger and Carson rifles have been shown and written about on a number of occasions. They are both of late Hawken period, being made about 1860, and reflect the style and workmanship of that period. The Modena rifle, however, definitely is of an earlier period, and reflects the workmanship and style of Jacob Hawken of about 1830-40. General Jones, who received this rifle from Modena, reported that it was purchased in 1833. After prolonged study, this writer is inclined to believe the General might have been mistaken by a year or two on his dates.

Modena went to the mountains in 1833. As he was originally from Taos, it is hardly likely that he obtained this particular rifle that first year. Much more likely is the premise that he had the rifle made while visiting St. Louis after one or two successful seasons in the mountains. The star inlays, and fancy patchbox indicate that the rifle was especially ordered, as opposed to a more ordinary Hawken of the period. The lack of engraving on an otherwise ornate rifle would indicate it was made before Tristam Campbell was available to contribute his talent for decorating the product of the Hawken shop. The rifle could have been obtained anytime between the years 1833 and 1842. It is our opinion that it was purchased by Modena the first summer he was able to get to St. Louis. A trip to St. Louis was a grand spree for the mountain man, and it took a good season in the mountains to finance the summer's fun. After months of drinking, rostering, and general hell raising, the trapper needed to gather his equipment and supplies, pick up the new rifle, and then get back to the mountains in time for the fall trapping. It was not an easy trip, and with the rendezvous well established to supply his needs, and furnish him a market, it took a very special reason to induce him to make such a trip. We submit that young Modena suffered through one or more seasons in the mountains with a less ornate rifle, before he was able to acquire the one displayed by the Colorado Historical Society in Denver.

We have touched upon the fur trade, its reason for being, its great expansion in our Rocky Mountains West during the early 1800's and its ultimate decline. Elsewhere in this volume, we have discussed the men who developed the rifle used in this trade, used to the extent that it is associated with the mountain men, even though it survived them by many years, and came to be used by those who succeeded them; scouts, hunters, adventurers, and emigrants.

Of no less importance, are the men who first used a rifle from the shop of Hawken; learned to depend upon it, came to swear by it, and who would have no other, if they could get a Hawken. Because no records were kept of sales, or numbers of rifles made and sold, or to whom, it is difficult in this day to determine who did, and who did not own a rifle known as the Hawken, or Hawkens, as it was commonly, if mistakenly, called. Sometimes we can identify the rifle held by the subject

of a painter, or photographer, or some scrap of record exists concerning repair, or new rifles made. Very rarely can we find documented proof that a particular rifle was owned by an individual. It may be that one generation says that so and so owned a particular rifle, and later generations accept it as fact, lacking proof otherwise. Certainly scant documentary evidence has been advanced to support the identification of many guns now accepted as having been owned by famous men. It has been said, and quite correctly, that most of our more famous western heroes must have been compulsive gun buyers, to have owned all the guns attributed to them.

A fine painting of Jim Baker is on display in the Historical Museum at Denver, Colorado. Baker is one of the better known mountain men, and at one time had a cabin and toll bridge across Clear Creek, at what is now the Tennyson Street crossing, in Denver. The full length picture of Baker shows him wearing buckskins, and holding the muzzle of a Hawken rifle, standing with its butt on the ground beside him. This particular rifle is shown equipped with a wear plate let into the forearm, much like the one found on the Modena rifle, exhibited in this same museum.

Hanging on the wall in the stairwell leading to the upper exhibit rooms of this same museum, is the portrait of Jim Bridger. "Old Gabe" as he was called, led a long and exciting life in the mountains, and became one of the best known of mountain men to the general public. Drawing upon the knowledge gained from years of trapping in the mountains, Bridger was able, in later years, to serve as guide and scout for various expeditions bent upon advancing civilization across the western plains and mountains.

Born in Richmond, Virginia, on March 17, 1804, Bridger came into the world at an opportune time. On the year of his birth, the major topic of conversation was the Lewis and Clark Expedition, and the events pertaining to it. Young Bridger's head was surely filled with the exciting thoughts of Indians, shining mountains, rivers and distant valleys. At the age of twelve, he moved with his parents to the vicinity of St. Louis, a location not likely to cause him to forget those boyish dreams. Even though he was apprenticed to a blacksmith, he did not lose the desire to see those shining mountains described so vividly by those who had accompanied Lewis and Clark.

When the Ashley-Henry Expedition left St. Louis on its way to establish a new innovation in fur-trading, young Bridger, age 18 years, was one of the men selected to become a free trapper, or Ashley man. When Hugh Glass became embroiled in a hand to hand conflict with a grizzly, with resulting wounds that caused death to seem eminent, young Bridger and a companion were selected to stay with him until death came, or he became able to travel. Fear of Indians, or of the unknown, whatever the reason, these two left the yet living Glass, taking his rifle and pouch, and rejoined their companions. The ultimate recovery of Glass, and his struggles to safety, and his later vow of revenge is an epic of western history. It is the only black mark on Bridger's record, and perhaps can be attributed to his tender years, and lack of confidence. His acts of later years certainly did much to erase this one blemish upon his record.

After General Ashley sold his interest in the Rocky Mountain Fur Company, various lieutenants of his acquired partnership in the venture. Bridger eventually became one of these partners, and remained one of the driving forces in this company until discontinuation of the rendezvous in 1839. After a continuous absence of seventeen years, he returned to St. Louis for a visit. But only for a visit; he soon returned to his beloved mountains! For nearly twenty years he had roamed the territory between Canada and southern Colorado, and between the Missouri River and the area now the states of Idaho and Utah. He was the first white man known to have visited Great Salt Lake, and later was to guide a party of Mormons to this place.

On the Oregon Trail in southwestern Wyoming, in 1843, he established Fort Bridger, which served as a way station for the pioneers headed for settlement in Oregon. In 1853, he was expelled from this post by the very Mormons he had helped, because they wanted a monopoly on this lucrative emigrant business. Once again forced out of business by overwhelming circumstances, Bridger retired, and returned to St. Louis. But retirement could not hold him, for he soon entered into government service, as scout and guide. In 1849, he had taken the Stansbury Railroad survey party to Utah, and in 1857-58 he conducted A. S. Johnston's Army Powder River Expedition. In 1865-66 he served as guide for the Bozeman Trail.

After long years of exposure to hardships and the elements, "Old Gabe" finally had to give up. With failing eyesight, and full of pain from old wounds and rheumatic joints, he retired again to his farm near Kansas City, Missouri, where he died on July 17, 1881.

"Kit" Carson, famous scout, guide and mountain man, gained his place in the first rank of the mountain men during the summer rendezvous of 1835. He had gone to California and back with Ewing Young in 1829-31, then had roamed widely as a free trapper. With Taos, New Mexico as home port, he had ranged the Great Plains, the Colorado Rockies, and the Uinta Basin. With a Bridger party, in the fall of 1834, he had gone into the Blackfoot country, where trappers could hardly go a mile from camp without being fired upon, but he had made a fairly good hunt and came to ren-

PLATE NO. 6

Kit Carson's Hawken rifle. This rifle is preserved in the Masonic Lodge, Santa Fe, New Mexico. Picture by C. T. Pearson

7

dezvous to await, with his restless companions, the arrival of the caravan from the States.

Here Carson had his famous duel. "On hand," Carson says, "was a large Frenchman, an overbearing kind of man, and very strong. He made a practice of whipping every man he was displeased with—and that was nearly all. One day, after he had beaten two or three men, he said he had no trouble to flog Frenchmen, and as for the Americans, he would take a switch and switch them.

"I did not like such talk from any man, so I told him I was the worst American in camp. There were many who could thrash him, but for the fact that they were afraid, and if he used such expressions any more, I would rip his guts."

"He said nothing, but started for his rifle, mounted his horse, and made his appearance in front of the camp. As soon as I saw this, I mounted my horse also, seized the first weapon I could get hold of, which was a pistol, and galloped up to him, demanding if I were the one he intended to shoot. Our horses were touching. He said no, drawing his gun at the same time, so he could have a fair shot at me. I was prepared and allowed him to draw his gun. We both fired at the same time, and all present said that but one report was heard. I shot him through the arm and his ball passed my head, cutting my hair and the powder burning my eye, the muzzle of his gun being near my head when he fired. During the remainder of our stay in camp we had no more bother with this French bully."

Samuel Parker seems to have witnessed this duel with Shunar, "the great bully of the mountains," and his description of the affair made Carson famous before he gained reputation through his association with Fremont in the 1840's. "Carson's ball," Parker observed, "entered Shunar's hand, came out at the wrist, and passed through the arm above the elbow. Shunar's ball passed over the head of Carson, and while he went for another pistol, Shunar begged that his life might be spared."

Carson's association with Brevet Capt. John C. Fremont began in midsummer of 1842. Carson was engaged to act as guide for Fremont's expedition, and the occasion was the beginning of a long and mutually profitable friendship.

While we are told that Hawken rifles, ammunition, blankets, cooking kettles, pack saddles, and other supplies were assembled for the trip, we cannot be sure what rifle Carson carried. Fremont reported after his path finding journey of 1842 through the far west, that Carson slept with a pair of 1836 Paterson Colts at half-cock by his head, and a Colt revolving rifle under the blanket beside him.

Carson is also credited with using Colt Paterson multishot cylinder rifles and Paterson revolvers in the battle with Kiowa and Commanche Indians who attacked a Santa Fe traders caravan in 1841. It would seem that the added firepower of the revolving rifles was recognized by Carson as being sufficient to equal the dependability and power of the St. Louis made Hawken.

Carson is credited with using a number of different rifles, by a number of different makers. He is claimed to have used rifles by Mills, Butler & Golcher, Whitney, and Colt, as well as having owned several Hawken rifles.

How many rifles he actually owned, and used is a matter for speculation, but it is known that manufacturers of that day were quick to claim their product to be the very favorite of any popular hero then in the public's eye. Carson's exploits had been publicized by writers of the period, and gun manufacturers were quick to get on the bandwagon. It mattered not whether Carson cared a whit for their rifle, if by connecting his name to their product, sales could be increased.

Carson owned a number of Hawken rifles, and one of these reposes in the museum of the Montazuma Lodge, AF&AM, Santa Fe, New Mexico. The illustrations in this chapter are of that rifle.

Carson was born in Madison County, Kentucky, December 24, 1809, but was reared on the Missouri frontier. He worked as a saddler's apprentice and teamster in the southwest, but in 1826, became a professional trapper, hunter and guide in the Rocky Mountain region. He accompanied John C. Fremont on his various journeys of exploration from 1842 to 1846. In 1853 he took part in the Mexican War, and later he became Indian agent at Taos, New Mexico. He resigned this post when the Civil War began, to help organize the First New Mexican Volunteer Infantry, and was commissioned a Lieutenant Colonel, eventually becoming a Brevet Brigadier General.

Illiterate, modest, and taciturn, he was remarkable for his exploits, but accounts of his life have often been glorified to suit fancy rather than fact. He died at Ft. Lyon, Colorado, May 23, 1868.

A contemporary of Carson, and an admirer of his, Thomas Tobin is another mountain man whom it is known owned a Hawken. Tobin's daughter married the son of Kit Carson. A picture of Tobin shows him dressed in a fine deerskin coat, and holding a long barreled Hawken rifle. John Barsotti, a Hawken authority in his own right, has reports that correspondence with the Tobin-Carson heirs has revealed this rifle to be lost, as has been the case with many such guns belonging to the participants of our western history.

CHAPTER 2

Jacob And Samuel Hawken, St. Louis Riflemakers

WHILE MOST magazine articles dealing with this subject have included a brief sketch of the lives of the men who developed and later perfected the style of rifle that came to be known as a Rocky Mountain Rifle, there are still a number of gaps in the continuity of the Hawken saga.

Of all the modern Hawken chroniclers, Horace Kephart probably had the best opportunity to get the complete story because of his friendship with J. P. Gemmer, and his acquaintance with some of the Hawken workmen, notably Charles Siever. Unfortunately, Kephart could not foresee the present day interest in Hawken rifles, and many of the questions that have arisen now, will perhaps, be forever unanswered.

Among those who are laid to rest in the tree-shaded serenity of Bellefontaine Cemetery, of St. Louis, Missouri, is the body of Samuel T. Hawken, famous rifle maker of that city. Placed there as a marker for his grave, and as a memorial to Sam and his older brother Jacob, the monument upon this grave pays silent tribute to these celebrated craftsmen. Beneath the likeness of a Rocky Mountain rifle, the following words are inscribed.

SAMUEL HAWKEN
Born October 26, 1792
Died May 9, 1884
Memorial and tribute to Samuel Hawken and
his brother Jacob Hawken 1786-1849
Makers of the famous "Hawken Rocky Mountain
and Plains Rifle" which for nearly half a
Century preceeding the Civil War was the
outstanding choice of the old mountain men,
trappers, and fur traders. General William
Ashley, the famous Scout Kit Carson, and
Buffalo Bill Cody were among the many of these
men who would have no other make if it was
possible to get a Hawken
Dedicated to his memory
With love by his grandsons
Frank S. Hawken, Sr.
and
Otis R. Hawken, Jr.

In the words of James E. Serven, the noted author and collector, who said, "The waters of the Mississippi have flowed past St. Louis many years now since sounds of activity could be heard from the Hawken shop facing toward the old levee—yet men from all parts of America still speak of those two master-craftsmen, Jake and Sam Hawken, with respect and admiration."

By establishing a gunshop in the village of St. Louis, in the year 1815, Jacob Hawken laid the foundation for a business that enjoyed a reputation for excellence for as long as the muzzle-loading rifle retained its importance upon the rapidly expanding frontier. Joined by his brother Samuel, in 1822, as these two produced rifles stamped J&S Hawken, St. Louis, their fame as rifle makers was spread wherever trappers and mountain men met. In their efforts to improve their product, new innovations were constantly being incorporated. When the patent, hooked breech came into use, it was promptly adopted by the Hawken shop. The long, full forestock was shortened and replaced by a metal rib and thimbles for the ram-rod, in the constant effort to promote sturdiness and durability. The upper tang was lengthened and tied to the long trigger bar with two screws passing through the wrist, thereby strengthening this, a notoriously weak area on a muzzle-loading rifle. As business prospered, more and more help wa added to the shop's working force. A system of production evolved whereas one man might work on only one component of the finished rifle, and it is through this simplified method of mass production that the identifying characteristics of the Hawken rifle emerged.

While no specimen of a flintlock Hawken rifle is known to exist, there is every probability that the early Hawken rifles were flintlocks. Flintlock rifles were common in the mountains as late as 1850, so this type of ignition was certainly not considered outmoded. Francis Parkman, author of the *"Oregon Trail,"* when writing of his adventures on the upper Platte in 1846, speaks of his guide, Henry Chatillon, and mentions that he, in preparing to go after a herd of buffalo, "primed his rifle afresh," so it would appear that Chatillon was armed with a flint-lock rifle. Parkman's own piece was a St. Louis rifle, of cap-lock ignition.

Lt. George Ruxton, the English officer who lived for

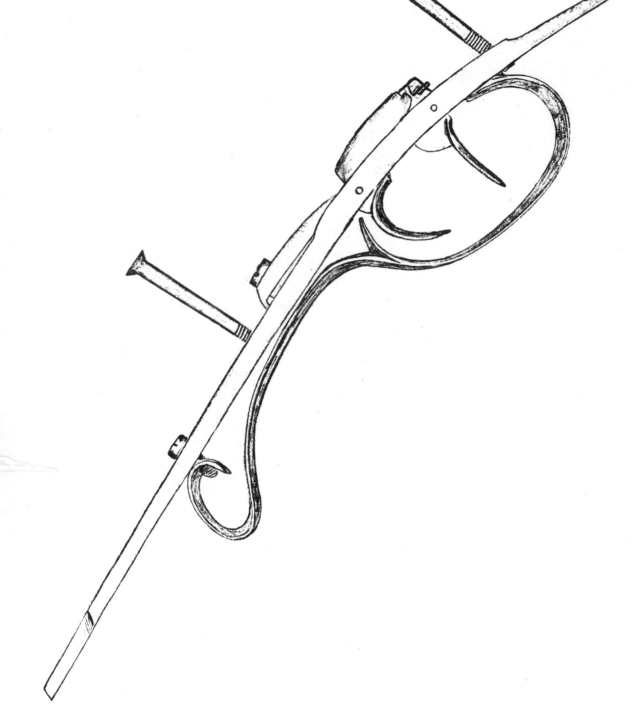

PLATE NO. 7

Right hand view of Hawken trigger. This feature, by being tied to upper tang with the two through bolts, rendered great strength to the wrist, a notoriously weak area of a muzzle-loading rifle. Drawing by C. T. Pearson

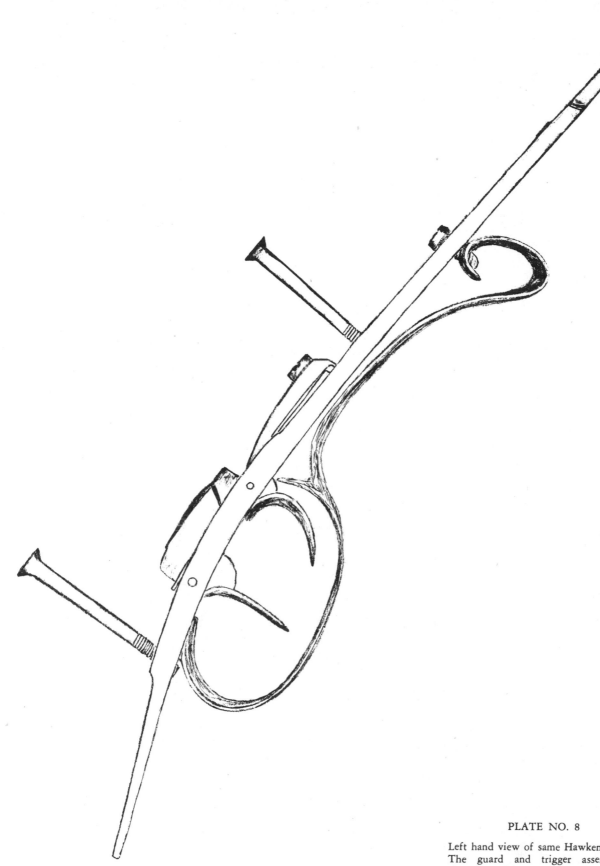

PLATE NO. 8

Left hand view of same Hawken trigger. The guard and trigger assembly is shown in full size, giving a graphic illustration of the amount of reinforcement it gave the wrist area. Drawing by C. T. Pearson

11

PLATE NO. 9

Samuel T. Hawken, noted riflemaker of Saint Louis, in his later years. Picture courtesy of Colorado State Historical Society Museum, Denver.

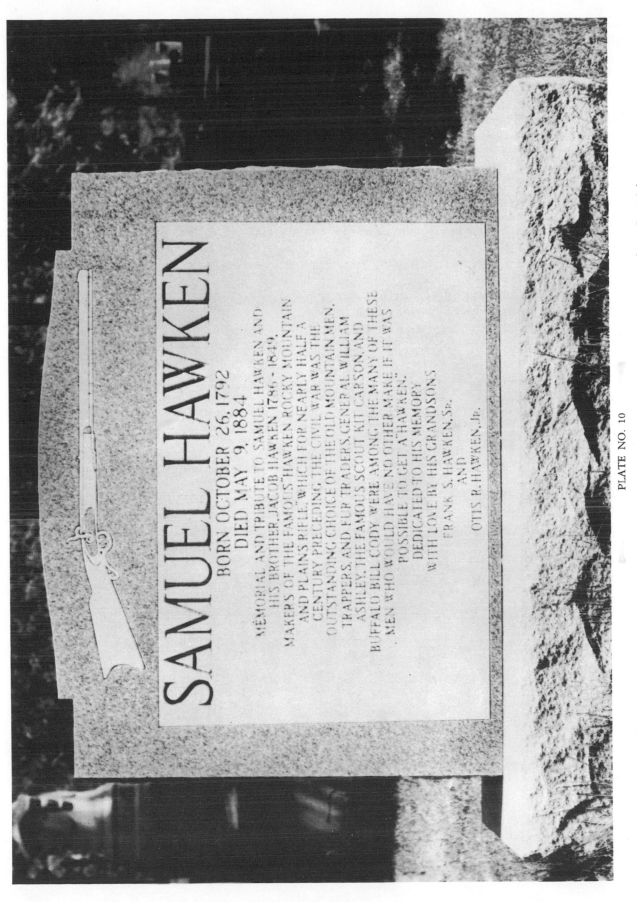

PLATE NO. 10

Memorial and grave marker of Samuel Hawken, Bellefontaine Cemetery, St. Louis. Picture by J. D. Baird

13

a time among the mountain men, and later wrote of his experiences in his book, *"Life In The Far West,"* describes his hero La Bonte's rifle as being from the shop of Hawken. Later in the story, he has William Drummond Stewart, the famous English sportsman, finding LaBonte and his friend Killbuck in desperate straits in the neighborhood of Independence Rock. His description reads—"They were gaunt and lantern-jawed, and clothed in tattered buckskin. Each held a rifle across his knees, but—strange sight in this country—one had its pan thrown open, which was rust eaten and contained no priming, the other's hammer was without a flint." Since he had described LaBonte's rifle being of Hawken manufacture, his reference here to the locks of these rifles would indicate that early Hawken rifles were of flintlock ignition.

Whether flint or percussion, the first Hawkens met with immediate favor with those who were going to the mountains, and the Hawken shop was launched into its role in the western trade.

The Missouri Historical Society Museum in St. Louis has a number of old City Directories in their Records Room, and it is in these volumes that we find the most accurate account of the Hawken shop. By 1838, the Hawken shop had grown to a small factory located at 31 Laurel Street, and with Sam in charge of a retail store at 35 Laurel.

Sometime between 1842 and 1845, the name of Laurel Street was changed to Washington Avenue, and thereafter we find the Hawken businesses listed at various addresses on Washington.

PLATE NO. 11

J&S Hawken advertisement, as appearing in the St. Louis City directories of 1842. Picture by J. D. Baird

A series of tragic events swept St. Louis in 1849. A cholera epidemic, much worse than previous ones that had scourged the city, was to take lives in such numbers that the bodies were cremated in the streets, in the effort to halt the epidemic. On May 8, 1849, Jacob Hawken became one of the victims of this epidemic.

In the summer of that same year, a fire, starting in a steamboat at the wharf, spread all through the other boats tied to the wharf, and into the city by way of Locust Street. A great number of buildings were burned, and others destroyed by blasting with explosives, in the efforts to bring the flames under control.

One of the business places burned out was that of Hoffman & Campbell, of 65 Locust Street. First mentioned in the 1842 Directory, Christian Hoffman and Tristam Campbell were listed as being employees of the Hawken factory. In 1845, they are listed as being in partnership at the address on Locust, and Christopher M. Hawken, son of Jacob Hawken, is listed as being at that addres with them.

PLATE NO. 12

H&C advertisement, as it appeared in the St. Louis City directories of 1842. Picture by J. D. Baird

Because the Hawken brothers would not sell under their name anything not made by them, it would appear that the Hoffman and Campbell business was a subsidiary of the Hawken shop, serving as a merchandising outlet for such items then in demand, but not handled at the Hawken store. Among such items would be Colt revolvers, Allen pistols, cheap Eastern rifles, and other trade goods. They also offered a full line of gunsmithing services.

Records show that Christopher Hawken left St. Louis

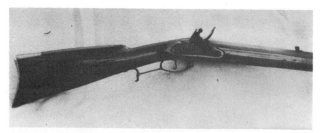

PLATE NO. 13

Early Pennsylvania flintlock rifle, of .50 caliber, very plain but stoutly built for frontier service. Very typical of those rifles carried by hunters and trappers who first penetrated the West. Early Hawken rifles followed this style, later trend was to shorter, more compact rifle. From the collection of T. K. Dawson. Picture by J. D. Baird

PLATE NO. 14

Flint lock by Ashmore. A number of Hawken percussion rifles are known to be equipped with locks by this maker. Ashmore, however, is better known for his fine flint locks, and early rifles by Jacob Hawken very likely were equipped with locks like this one. From the collection of T. K. Dawson. Picture by J. D. Baird

after the death of Jacob, and went West. The 1854 Directory shows that Tristam Campbell, former partner of Hoffman, is listed as partner to Sam Hawken. Samuel's son, William S. Hawken is also listed as being with Sam—this being the first indication that William S. had entered the gun business. In this same directory is the information that Christian Hoffman and Christopher Hawken are partners in a livery business at 13

PLATE NO. 15

Ornate mountain style rifle marked T. Campbell on top flat of barrel, St. Louis on back action lock. Having access to same source of supply as Hawken shops, Campbell used those parts he was familiar with, but his style of engraving, profuse use of silver, and other features mark this as his rifle, and not one of Hawken manufacture. From the collection of Wm. Almquist. Picture by J. D. Baird

PLATE NO. 16

Top view of the tang, breech area of the rifle marked T. Campbell. Note two silver bands in breech, a trademark of Tristam Campbell. Tang is very similar to those found on several J&S Hawken rifles, as is also the breech. Campbell worked alone after 1859, but details of hardware on this rifle suggest it could have been made in 1845-50 period. From the collection of Wm. Almquist. Picture by J. D. Baird

PLATE NO. 17

Cheekpiece view of T. Campbell rifle. Panelled area around cheekpiece appears on late S. Hawken marked rifles, suggesting that Campbell helped stock these rifles, while working as partner to Samuel Hawken. Again note use of silver. From the collection of Wm. Almquist. Picture by J. D. Baird

and 14 Market Street. While Hoffman is not believed to have had strong ties to the gun business, Campbell was a good gunsmith and a fine engraver, whose speciality was in embellishing rifles constructed by others. The 1859 Directory lists him as being in business alone at 76 Locust Street, and the Hawken business being in the name of Sam's son, William S. Hawken.

By 1859, Samuel's health had deteriorated to the point where he, leaving his son William S. to dispose of the St. Louis business, left that city on April 20th, to travel to Denver, Colorado.

Arriving in Denver on June 30, 1859, Sam is reported to have briefly tried his hand at gold mining, but soon gave it up and turned his hand to his old trade, that of making guns. In January 1860, he opened shop in Denver, and February 15, the Rocky Mountain News carried an advertisement to the effect that he was prepared to manufacture his style of rifle to order. In addition, he was prepared to do light iron work of all kinds, as well as make and repair door keys, and repair instruments of all kinds.

On April 18, this same newspaper carried the following news item:

"Our venerable friend, S. Hawken, whose rifles for years have had an unequalled celebrity among the hunters, trappers, and voyageurs of the plains and mountains, has raised a tall pole in front of his shop on Ferry Street, on the top of which a mammoth rifle is swinging on a pivot. The big gun can be seen from all parts of the city—now pointing at the mountains, now away from them as it is swayed in the breeze.

Mr. Hawken is an old resident of St. Louis —having made guns there for 35 years; he came to this country about a year ago for the benefit of his health, which he informs us has been completely restored, a result which he attributes to our unequalled climate."

This writer knows of no S. Hawken rifles marked Denver, Colorado, but there have been references to rifles marked W. S. Hawken, Denver, Colorado. This is, of course, those rifles marked by William S. Hawken, who continued Sam's Denver shop, after Sam retired and returned to St. Louis.

William S. had remained in St. Louis until he was able to dispose of the Hawken interests there. City directories of 1859-60 contain the following advertisement.

WILLIAM L. WATT
Successor to W. S. Hawken
Rifle & Shotgun Manufacture
21 Washington Ave.
Hawken rifles always on hand.

Watt probably had the controlling interest in the business, but it is believed that a man named Eterle and John Phillip Gemmer also had an interest. Horace Kephart stated that Gemmer bought the business in 1862, but city directories still list Watt as proprietor as late as 1864, and it is not until 1866 that Gemmer is listed as owner. In all probability, Gemmer was unable to purchase full ownership before this date. The shop remained in Gemmer's hands until he closed it in 1915.

It goes without saying that Samuel Hawken's life was unique in a number of ways. Entering into the gunsmithing business in St. Louis, as he did in 1822, he saw the complete transition from the flintlock era through the caplock period, and witnessed the ultimate replacement of muzzle-loading arms with the powerful breech-loading repeaters that are the immediate parents of todays weapons. Samuel Hawken played no small part in this era, and Hawken standards for accuracy, power, sturdiness, and dependability were not easily matched by the breechloading rifle that eventually replaced the muzzle-loading rifle as a serious hunting and defense weapon. During the hey-day of this famous St. Louis rifle, the name Hawken was synonymous with quality.

Samuel Hawken's lifespan witnessed a great number

PLATE NO. 18

The last rifle made by Samuel Hawken—displayed in the Missouri Historical Society Museum, St. Louis. Made up of components consisting of boughten barrel, lock, cast trigger guard, forend tip, escutcheons and rear sight, it is far cry from handmade rifles of earlier days. Having all the attributes of rifles made by J. P. Gemmer, it very likely was assembled by Sam from ready-made parts, with a minimum of hand work. Gemmer told Horace Kephart that Sam sold his rifle to a Mr. Charles F. Filley. Courtesy of Missouri Historical Society. Picture by J. D. Baird

PLATE NO. 19

Close up of the breech of Sam's last rifle. Kephart does not tell us when Sam made this rifle—only that it was in his old age. Probably between 1865 and 1870. Note the sloping upper edge of lock, where it flows into carved outline of lock section, a feature found on S. Hawken marked rifles attributed to Gemmer, who continued Hawken quality and tradition. Courtesy of Missouri Historical Society. Picture by J. D. Baird

of important events in our nation's history. Among these might be mentioned the rise, the tremendous growth, and the decline of the steamboat as a mode of transportation. Being of a migrating spirit himself, he would have particularly noted the great westward flow of people, homeseekers, as they tamed and built across lands that once contained nothing but buffalo and the Indian. In his papers is found the remark that in 1849, Denver was a great metropolis, as compared to St. Louis when he arrived there in 1822. He saw this little village grow from a hamlet on the river bank to a great, thriving city, and contributed his share in that growth. It is fitting that such a man be remembered and honored by the monument dedicated to him.

CHAPTER 3

Early Hawken Rifle

UPON CLOSE examination of the accompanying illustrations, it will be seen that the rifle discussed here is a very early example of the work of Jacob and Samuel Hawken. While unquestionably genuine, it has a number of features that conflict with popular concepts of what is characteristically Hawken.

Because there is no information concerning the history of the piece, or its original owner, there is a lot of room for speculation as to the reasons for its being. Indeed most Hawken rifles leave room for speculation as to their history, date of manufacture, previous owners, and so forth. However, keeping in mind known facts concerning the Hawken brothers and their product, certain deductions can be made.

On all Hawken rifles examined, and pictures of Hawken rifles studied, it was noted that the breech section gave good clues to the age of the rifle. The most important single thing in any rifle is dependable ignition and the Hawken shop gave much attention to this detail of construction. The nipple seat, and surrounding snail area was steadily improved until by the time Sam was ready to retire, it had become as nearly perfect as was possible to obtain.

Using this constant attempt at improvement, as a guide, it is possible to put any particular rifle into an age bracket. By also utilizing other known features as well, it is possible to pin this time down to possibly a decade or less. In this rifle's case, we have placed the date of manufacture somewhere within the period between 1825 and 1830.

The percussion system was developed in the early 1820's and caught on fast in the West. The rifle shown is equipped with a very early style of snail, but the shape of this arrangement is not good, as the cap flashed all over the place, with resultant corrosion. Later Hawkens had this fault corrected, and it was improved again and again until the ultimate perfection found in Sam's last rifle. Plate No. 25 shows that in this case, the nipple flash and resultant corrosion has very nearly obliterated the name stamped on the barrel.

Most Hawken rifles are stamped on the upper barrel flat, behind the rear sight. Name stamps varied from time to time. Some are marked J. Hawken, St. Louis,

others marked J. & S. Hawken, St. Louis and some just S. Hawken, St. Louis. A few, like the Horace Kephart Hawken, are left unmarked, and there are variations in the stamps themselves. A number of stamps were employed over the years, one being replaced by a new one as it became too worn to leave a clear impression. When J. P. Gemmer bought the Hawken shop after

PLATE NO. 20

Archie Peterson, of Gowrie, Iowa, holding his very early J&S Hawken rifle. This rifle is now in the Leonard collection. This could easily be the earliest Hawken rifle still in existence. Picture by J. D. Baird

PLATE NO. 21

Patchbox lid of iron, with crudely engraved standing elk. Engraving is suggestive of T. Campbell's early work, but rifle is of a period preceding that in which Campbell is recorded as being in Hawken shop. Patchbox could have been installed at a later date. Picture by J. D. Baird

PLATE NO. 22

Patchbox with lid open. Lid spring is missing, but was secured to bottom of cavity, with extension pressing on lid. Pressure on thumb catch on upper edge of lid would allow lid to spring open. Picture by J. D. Baird

Sam's retirement, he made free use of the Hawken stamp, as well as his own. It is certain that some of the rifles in existence today and marked S. Hawken, were in reality, made by Gemmer, as he continued the Haw- ken tradition for as long as making and selling such rifles continued to be profitable.

Again studying Plate No. 25, it will be seen that on the rifle being discussed here, that the name J & S

19

PLATE NO. 23

Cheekpiece with silver plate. Note bottom line of cheekpiece. Suggestive of the beavertail form of cheekpiece of later rifles. Picture by J. D. Baird

HAWKEN is used, but without the word St. Louis, as is common on most Hawken rifles. Upon close examination, it becomes apparent that the name is applied with individual letter stamps, as opposed to a machine stamp, as the slight unevenness of the letters will reveal. It would seem that this rifle was built before the Hawken brothers had obtained a machine stamp with which to mark their product.

As the Hawken shop grew, it took on more and more help, and rifles became more and more standardized. But when Jake and Sam were occasionally shoeing a horse to make a buck, they had the time to build a rifle just like the customer wanted. A customer is always

right; especially if you need his business. If he wanted a fancy rifle, you can bet he got the fanciest they were capable of building at that time. Many years later, they made much better and much more handsome rifles. It takes many rifles and several years of experience to gain the skill that makes this possible.

Early J & S Hawkens were usually full-stocked weapons, but half-stock, ribbed models were fast gaining acceptance. Sam even made full-stock models rather late in his career. Probably on special order. But, it was the half-stock model that was to reach such heights of esteem with such men as Bridger and Modena.

The use of oval escutcheons to protect the wood

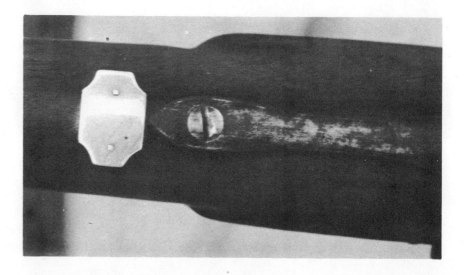

PLATE NO. 24

Short tang and silver ornament of same size and shape of barrel key escutcheons. Picture by J. D. Baird

PLATE NO. 25

Top view of breech area, showing name stamp. J&S Hawken is faintly discernable, but erosive action from capflash has nearly obliterated stamp. Picture by J. D. Baird

around the barrel retaining keys is almost a trademark of Hawken. However, they were not always used on the full-stocked models. It is believed that there may have been a transition period before the exclusive use of the oval shaped escutcheons were finally adopted. On the particular rifle shown here, it will be seen that the escutcheons are variants of what is usually considered standard Hawken style. This writer believes that they are a part of that transition period, and are a forerunner of the oval shape that was so universally used on later Hawken rifles. Made of German silver, they are not inletted, but nailed directly to the surface with silver nails. A plate of the same size and shape is similarly fastened to the top of the wrist immediately behind the tang. Plate No. 24 shows this detail to good effect.

Another notable feature of this rifle is the deviation found pertaining to the trigger and trigger guard assembly. One of the features of a Hawken was the one piece trigger bar with the scroll guard secured to it. This rifle has a variation on this theme in that the trigger is a separate unit, very like early Penn. rifles, and is held in place by the trigger guard, when it is drawn up tight against the stock, again as is the case with the Penn. rifle. The trigger is double set, in that the rear trigger must be set, for the front trigger to work. In inspecting the trigger guard, it was apparent that the bow and decorative frontpiece is from a shotgun guard, with the conventional scroll welded to it.

Since the Hawken shop is known to have assembled shotguns from parts secured from Belgium, as was common practice among gunsmiths of that era, it is easy to see what took place. It is a simple thing to attach an easily bent scroll to a ready made bow, and in

a few moments have an engraved trigger guard ready to install. By studying the different views of this rifle, it will be noted that some attempt was made to make it rather decorative. It would appear that this rifle was in all probability built to order for a hunter who wished something a little finer than the ordinary run of rifles.

The generous use of silver on this rifle is noteworthy, since later Hawkens were nearly always very plain, and always iron mounted. Silver reflects light a long way on the prairie, and the Mountain Men in hostile country soon learned to shy away from such foo-fa-ral.

In Plate No. 23 we again see the use of silver for ornamentation. This inlay shows engraving vastly superior to that on the patch-box, and is very similar to ones found in Tryon's catalog. It is believed that this ornament was obtained through such a supply house. The inlay is let into the wood, and secured in place by two silver nails. There are thirteen stars surrounding the eagle. Also noteworthy is the position of the eagle's head. It is said that if the eagle is looking toward the arrows, it means war, and if he should be facing the ivy, it would denote peace.

Notice too, that the cheekpiece shown in Plate No. 23 is another deviation from usual Hawken style. Some of the early Hawken rifles use a cheekpiece very nearly like those found on Tenn. rifles, and later went to the wide, flat beaver tail form. Another indication that this rifle is a transition piece is the semi-beaver tail shape of the cheekpiece. Not really a beaver tail, yet having line and shape that would indicate that a new trend was being developed.

Hawken rifles that are equipped with patch boxes of any kind are rather rare, so it was with great interest that we examined this one. Oval in shape, made of

21

PLATE NO. 26

View of lock and breech. Note nipple lug was originally equipped with clean out screw, but this feature has been broken. Lock is marked R. Kingsland & Co., Warranted. Picture by J. D. Baird

PLATE NO. 27

Top view of rear sight. While later Hawken rifles retained the general shape of upright portion of sight, the base was gradually shortened. Picture by J. D. Baird

PLATE NO. 28

Forearm of Peterson rifle, showing nailed on barrel key escutcheons of silver. Picture by J. D. Baird

PLATE NO. 29

Lower thimble of Peterson rifle. Note use of two pins holding this fixture in place. Picture by J. D. Baird

PLATE NO. 30

Toeplate of Peterson's Hawken rifle. Held in place with four iron screws, it is lightly engraved. Picture by J. D. Baird

sheet iron, it is very simple in construction, but sturdy and the patch compartment is of generous proportions. The lid is hinged on the lower edge, and is kept closed by a very simple spring clasp on the upper edge. Of particular note is the engraving upon the surface of the lid. Depicting an elk, the quality of engraving leads one to think of Ruxton's description of LaBonte's rifle. "And the only ornament was an exceedingly ferocious buffalo, not very artistically engraved upon the trap in the stock." A flat spring within the patch compartment, and bearing on the under side of the lid makes the lid self-opening whenever the spring clasp is released. All very simple, yet sturdy and dependable.

The toe-plate is of iron, lightly engraved, and held in place by four screws. Here again we find the quality of engraving better than that found on the patch box, and it is assumed that this piece too, came from outside the shop. Fittings such as these were stock items from such supply houses as Tryon and others.

Probably the most unusual feature of the rifle is the shape of the lockplate. Careful examination of the lock and wood surrounding it will confirm that the lock has been part and parcel of the rifle ever since it left the Hawken shop many, many years ago. Hanson, in his book "The Plains Rifle", reports on good authority that the Hawken shop purchased both barrels and locks on more than one occasion. The lockplate is marked "B. Kingsland, Warranted" and this writer has been unable to learn whether this refers to the manufacturer or the jobber who sold it.

Most descriptions of a Hawken rifle describe the sights as consisting of a slanting buckhorn rear and a silver blade front sight set into a copper base. This

writer has seen Hawken rifles with this type of front sight, and he has also found Hawkens with the silver blade set into an iron base. On occasion one is found with the blade set directly into the barrel. Such is the case with the rifle being discussed. The front sight is 3/4 of an inch long and stands 3/16 of an inch high. As can be seen in Plate 27, the rear sight is traditional Hawken slanting buckhorn, peened into a shallow mortise in the barrel, and capable of being moved right or left for sight correction, should the need arise.

The barrel of this rifle is 33 5/16 inches long and measures 1 inch across the flats at the muzzle. It measures 1 1/16 inches across the flats at the breech. Present caliber is .58 but it should be remembered that this barrel has probably been recut several times and quite likely was nearer to .52 or .53 caliber, when new. Overall length of the rifle is 49 3/4 inches and total weight is 10 1/2 lbs. The ramrod guide and lower ferrule are of iron and are traditional Hawken styling. The barrel is secured to the stock with two iron keys and is equipped with hook breech to facilitate removal of the barrel for cleaning.

In summing up, we will see that we have here a very unusual specimen. Made very early after the partnership between Jacob and Samuel was formed, it reflects some of the Eastern influence of the times, yet shows strong characteristics of the rifles that were to come out of the Hawken shop for many years. As improvements were developed, they became part of the rifle, and this constant search for durability and dependability put Hawken in the forfront among riflemakers for the Western trade, and kept them there as long as muzzle loading arms used for hunting and Indian fighting.

CHAPTER 4

Full Stock Hawken Rifles

THE FIREARMS collection of the late Orville Dunham, of Decatur, Illinois, had in it a very fine J & S Hawken fullstock rifle. Possibly of the 1835 to 1845 period, it is very typical of fullstock rifles produced in the Hawken shop. While it was the half-stocked, ribbed models that came to be so widely acclaimed, the Hawken brothers made many full-stocked rifles. Sam even made full-stocks on special order rather late in his career as gunmaker. A great proportion of the early rifles produced by the Hawken shop is believed to have been full-stocks, but because of the severe conditions under which they were used, their survival rate is very low.

The rifle being discussed here is an extremely nice piece, somewhat shorter than a Pennsylvania rifle, but greatly resembling that style. Stocked in lightly stripped hard maple, with a 36 1/2 inch barrel 1 and 1/32 inches across the flats, the rifle measures 54 inches overall, and weighs 10 1/4 lbs. Of .50 cal., it is iron mounted, with conventional scroll guard and double set triggers. There is no patchbox, and the only ornament is a small engraved ring of coin silver set into the Tenn. style cheekpiece.

The barrel of this rifle is secured to the stock with three retaining keys. The heads of these keys are of rectangular shape and escutcheons to protect the wood were not used. These keys are not slotted for retaining pins, as is the case with later rifles. The front sight is the oft described silver blade set into a copper base. The rear sight is also conventional, being the low slanting buckhorn, but of slightly earlier design than that found on later rifles. The barrel is stamped on the top flat, midway between the breech and rear sight, the name J & S Hawken, St. Louis. The rifling consists of seven wide lands and narrow grooves, with a twist of one turn in 48 inches.

The barrel is equipped with a patent breech, but this is not of the hooked variety. The patent breech

PLATE NO. 31

Mr. Baird examining the .50 caliber fullstock J&S Hawken rifle from the Orville Dunham collection. Picture by J. D. Baird

and 5 1/2 inch tang are of one piece construction, with the nipple set into the sloping face atop the semi-scroll snail. The nipple sets at somewhat of a steep angle, and it will be seen in Plate No. 32 that some difficulty was experienced in getting this particular hammer to strike it correctly. The purpose of setting the nipple at this angle was to serve two purposes. First, the nipple could be easily removed, with the hammer at full cock, without the necessity of removing the lockplate, so that the nipple wrench could properly engage the nipple. Secondly, the easiest and quickest way to clean such a piece is to up-end it and pour hot water through the bore. With this particular angle of nipple, the stream of water exiting from the nipple would pass over the hammer in its full cock position. The only thing left to do then was to shake the remaining drops of water from the piece and wipe it dry while warm from the hot water treatment. A steeper angle of nipple, and the hammer could not be made to fall on it correctly. A lesser angle and the stream of water exit-

ing from the nipple would strike the hammer face, unless the lock was removed while cleaning. The proper angle is very desirable, but this writer knows from experience that it is difficult to get the hammer to properly strike the nipple.

Ned Roberts, in his book, *"The Muzzle-Loading Caplock Rifle"* talks at some length on the development and use of the patent breech. Repeating his words here would serve no useful purpose, but this writer would like to point out that most writers have seemingly overlooked one very important facet in this respect. Aside from being stronger than the conventional drum and nipple, it serves two very important functions. The least of these is the protection it offers the lock and barrel from the corrosive action of the cap-flash. Most important is the ease of cleaning it affords. With no corners and crevices as is the case with the drum and nipple, there is nothing to retain moisture, and with the hot water treatment described above, drying is quick and sure. Within minutes after cleaning,

PLATE NO. 32

Breech view of J&S Hawken fullstock percussion rifle from Dunham collection. Picture by J. D. Baird

25

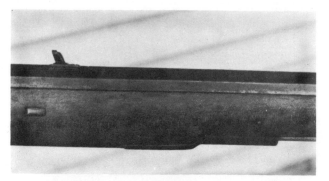

PLATE NO. 33

Rear sight and lower thimble of Dunham rifle. Picture by J. D. Baird

PLATE NO. 34

Business end of the Orville Dunham Hawken rifle. Picture by J. D. Baird

PLATE NO. 35

Detail of front sight on Dunham rifle. Picture by J. D. Baird

the rifle is ready to be reloaded; an important point when camped in Indian country with its ever present hazard of attack from hostiles.

The lock of this rifle is marked J & S Hawken, with

some decorative engraving upon its surface. It is very similar to the Powell locks sometimes found on Hawken rifles and pistols, and it could be that the lock and hammer for this rifle came from that source. Powell & Co. were St. Louis hardware dealers. It is most unusual to find the Hawken name on the lock of one of their guns, although locks of their own manufacture sometimes had, on the inside surface, the name of the workman who made it.

The lockplate is held in place by a single lockbolt, and the head of this bolt is supported by a small teardrop shaped piece of iron let into the wood. The lockbolt head is not countersunk into this inlay, as is often the case with later rifles.

As stated above, the trigger assembly is of conventional Hawken styling. Note, however, that the shape of the scroll is that of the early full circle, as opposed to the more oval form found on later rifles. Not often is the retaining screw found extending into the center of this scroll, as is found on this particular rifle. Perhaps this screw is a replacement, but it appears to be original, so perhaps there are others. The bow of the guard is of thinner dimensions than found on later guards, and has a more pronounced circular form. This style of guard is generally found on early Hawken rifles, and is one of the many small things used in attempting to date any particular specimen. Another feature not noted on other rifles is that the trigger adjustment screw is double slotted, to facilitate adjustment with the point of a knife blade.

The buttplate of this rifle is of iron, with shallow crescent. While of slightly different configuration than the plate on the halfstock Hawken in the Peterson collection, its method of manufacure is the same. A faint line of brass is visible in the juncture of the crescent and heel, showing it was shaped and forged by hand. This buttplate measures 4 1/2 inches from toe to heel and 1 1/2 inches across its widest point. The top piece extends up the stock 3 1/8 inches.

The toeplate is also of iron, of typical Pennsylvania styling, held in place by three iron screws. It is 4 1/2 inches in length, and is 5/8ths of an inch in width. There is no engraving, or any attempt at decoration.

The forend tip, ramrod guides and lower thimble are also of iron, again with no attempt at decoration. Indeed, the lower thimble is even plainer than those found on other and later Hawken rifles, being 3 1/2 inches long. Half of this being the thimble, and the balance being the tail piece. The inside diameter of the ramrod guides is slightly over .45 caliber, and they are 1 5/8 inches in length.

The stock of this rifle, in comparison to most Hawken rifles, is very slim, being very like that of the Pennsylvania and Tennessee style rifles. The workmanship is excellent, with very good fitting of metal to

Rear sight on the Hawken rifle in the Louer collection. The prongs of this "buckhorn" sight nearly come together at the top, forming a large, easily discernable aperature. This sight would be very effective in snap shooting at charging target. Picture by E. Louer

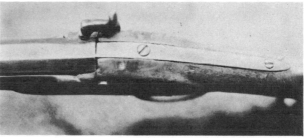

PLATE NO. 38

The Louer rifle, unlike the Dunham Hawken rifle, used a Kentucky style breech plug, with long tang. The nipple lug is formed on the barrel, rather than on a patent breech. Picture by E. Louer

PLATE NO. 39

View of the lock mortise of the Hawken rifle in the Louer collection. Picture by E. Louer

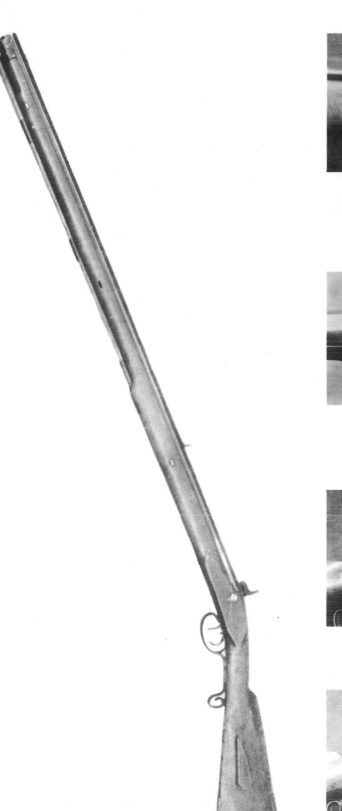

PLATE NO. 36

Fullstock J&S Hawken rifle in Louer collection. Picture by E. Louer

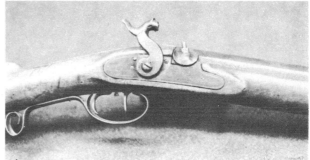

PLATE NO. 40

View of lock section of Mr. Louer's fine fullstock Hawken rifle. Stock is maple. Picture by E. Louer

wood throughout. The comb of the stock terminates in the conventional Hawken style, that of the sharp rounded edge where it drops into the wrist.

While all Hawken rifles followed a recognizable style, there is a great deal of variation among individual rifles. Conditions changed rapidly during the Hawken epoch, and Hawken rifles show a steady trend of conformation to these changing conditions. It was this constant effort on the part of the Hawken shop, to produce the best rifle possible, that put them in the forefront among rifle builders, and kept them there in spite of competition from much larger firms who were also making rifles for the western trade.

Another fine fullstock rifle of this period is in the collection of Edwin Louer, of Tucson, Arizona. Differing only in minor construction details, it too is very typical of those full stocked rifles made in the Hawken shop.

While we do not have measurements and other specifications of such nature that are of particular interest to the builder, the accompanying plates will explain the features of this rifle. This form of breech is often found in such rifles, and while not as intricate, or as ornate, as those found on later rifles, it is very functional, and exceedingly easy to keep clean. Such simplicity is indicative of the Hawken shop's efforts to produce a sturdy, functional rifle that could be depended upon, under difficult conditions, and for extended periods far from any source of repair.

CHAPTER 5

Mariano Modena's Rifle

Rocky Mountain News, April 18, 1860 (Page 3, col. 2)

Our venerable friend, S. Hawken, whose rifles for years have had an unequalled celebrity among the hunters, trappers, and voyageurs of the plains and mountains has raised a tall pole in front of his shop on Ferry Street, on the top of which a mammoth rifle is swinging on a pivot. The big gun can be seen from all parts of the city—now pointing at the mountains, now away from them, as it is swayed in the breeze.

Mr. Hawken is an old resident of St. Louis—having made guns there for 35 years; he came to this country about a year ago for the benefit of his health, which he informs us has been completely restored, a results which he attributes to our unequalled climate."

THAT SAMUEL Hawken was a man of some importance in Denver is readily discerned by the number of references to him in the old issues of Denver's oldest newspaper, *"The Rocky Mountain News."* Having left St. Louis on April 20, 1859, he arrived in Denver June 30th, and in January of the following year, he opened a gun shop on Ferry Street.

On February 15, 1860, the *Rocky Mountain News* carried the following advertisement;

3:5 adv.

"S. Hawken, for the last thirty-seven years engaged in the manufacture of the Rocky Mountain rifle in St. Louis, would respectfully say to the citizens of Denver, Auraria, and to his old mountain friends, that he has established himself in the gun business on Ferry St., between Fourth nd Fifth, next door to Jones & Cartwrights, Auraria, and is now prepared to manufacure his style of rifle to order.

N. B. In addition to the above, he is prepared to do light iron work of all kinds. Door keys made and repaired. Instruments also repaired."

Because Sam had been in Denver from July of 1859 to January of the following year before he opened his shop, he must have needed the time to find quarters for his shop, and have a stock of supplies sent to him from St. Louis. As he planned to continue making his style of rifle, it would be much simpler to have the components shipped to him from the old Hawken factory, than it would to fabricate everything in his small shop. He may have taken such supplies with him on his trip out, and it simply took him that long to find quarters. In his letters, he speaks of the scarcity of sawed lumber for building in the rapidly growing city of Denver.

This writer knows of no S. Hawken rifles stamped Denver, Colorado, but there has been reference to rifles marked W. S. Hawken, Denver Col. This, of course, would be rifles marked by William S. who continued Sam's Denver shop, after Sam had returned to St. Louis. The April 4th, 1862 issue of the *Rocky Mountain News* carried this news item—

"Mr. Hawken, son of the worthy and well known Uncle Samuel, of Hawken rifle notoriety, the Western world over, has removed his gun shop to F. Street, sign of the Big Gun, where everybody can have their guns and pistols put in order, on sure and scientific principles. Ed."

Perhaps it is a vague point, but one worthy of consideration; barrels made in the Hawken factory in St. Louis, and sent to Sam in Denver were marked St. Louis at the factory. Sam, and later William S., stamped their name on the barrel if they installed it in a rifle.

The only Hawken rifle in the Colorado Historical Museum at Denver is the one formerly owned by the famed hunter and Indian scout Mariano Modena. This rifle has been illustrated and described in several articles, by different researchers, but this writer feels that there are some details concerning this rifle that have not been explored in depth.

Mariano Modena was born in Taos, and was of mixed blood; being three fourths Mexican and one fourth Indian. He received an education from the Spanish Priests, and it is said that he spoke thirteen Old World languages, read in five more, and later learned to speak a dozen Indian dialects.

Although Modena was reported as having an enduring hatred of all Indians, he married a Flathead girl, named her John, and promptly set her up in business.

Having long admired the Big Thompson Valley in Colorado, he built a fort there and named it Namaqua. When the westward bound wagon trains started coming through there, he built a toll bridge. Mountain men dropped in from time to time, and there seemed

PLATE NO. 41

Rifle on top: an original S. Hawken rifle; center rifle, copy of top rifle, made by Ed White; bottom rifle, copy of Modena rifle by Ed White. Photo by J. D. Baird.

always enough of his old friends about to defend and run the establishment, with John in general charge of everything. As for Modena, he was constantly ranging the mountains and plains, using the ranch and fort only as a home base. A place to replenish supplies and occasionally indulge in a home-cooked meal.

When the Overland Stage was put into operation, Fort Namaqua became a stage station on this route.

General A. H. Jones is quoted to the effect that shortly before Modena's death, he presented his favorite Hawken rifle to the General, along with the admonishment, "Keep her clean, General!"

There is a great deal of controversy being expressed among Hawken enthusiasts, concerning the date given on the silver plate in the cheekpiece of this rifle. A number of details on the rifle are of conflicting nature, and some confusion exists as to what might be the proper explanation. The author made a special trip to Denver expressly to view this rifle, and while there, formed his own theory on the problem. He offers it in this discussion for what it is worth.

The writer will not dispute the 1833 date given as date of purchase by Modena. The characteristics of the buttplate, trigger guard, escutcheons, shape of stock, and type of wood, all place the stock in the 1830 to 1840 period. J & S Hawken rifles of that period are often found stocked in walnut, as is the Modena rifle. It is the barrel and lock that offer the most points of conflict, and a logical explanation appears upon close study of these points.

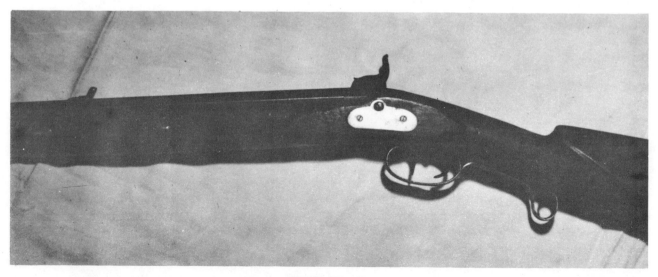

PLATE NO. 42

Cheekpiece side of Modena rifle. Courtesy of Colorado Historical Museum. Picture by J. D. Baird

Mariano Modena took great pride in this particular rifle. He had a number of Hawken rifles, but this one is recorded as being his favorite. References describe it as being of .50 caliber originally, and this would be in line with what was generally considered the favorite caliber for that period. The silver stars, and plain iron patchbox would indicate it was purchased before Tristam Campbell went to work for the Hawken shop. That would explain the lack of engraving found on later Hawken rifles that show attempts at embellishment.

When Sam opened his shop in Denver, Mariano Modena had been using this rifle for some 25 years, under conditions that in all probability, would cause it to show signs of extreme wear. Being a favorite rifle, it is reasonable to expect him to prefer having this rifle repaired, rather than replace it. Sam's proximity in Denver would further facilitate having such a desire fulfilled. A new barrel, of a larger caliber for the now important buffalo, a new lock and possibly new works in the triggers, would completely restore the old rifle.

Fitting a new barrel to an old rifle would pose no particular problems to a gunsmith of Sam's ability. The fact that it was of slightly larger dimensions than the old one would mean relieving the barrel channel a bit. The very thin wood on the forearm indicates that this was done carefully and neatly.

Absence of corrosion on the patent breech would indicate that this, too, was part of the new barrel, and that considerable skill was exercised in fitting the new breech to the old tang. Absence of nicks and scratches, and the sharpness of the barrel flats all show the probability that the barrel is of later date than is the stock. Indeed, the hardware of the stock shows a great deal more wear and age than does the barrel and breech.

The rear sight is somewhat unusual in shape. It is not at all what one usually encounters on a S. Hawken barrel, and most likely has been transferred from the old barrel. Directly behind the rear sight, and centered perfectly on the barrel flat are the words, "St. Louis." Further down the barrel than usual, and cut at a distinct angle to line of bore, is the name "S. Hawken." This feature alone is worth comment, because this writer has not encountered such a sloppy job of barrel stamping on a S. Hawken barrel before. Another reason to believe the St. Louis was applied at the factory, and that Sam put his stamp on after installing the barrel!

The barrel is about .58 caliber, and what appears to be funneling of the muzzle is a deliberate Hawken feature described elsewhere. The front sight is the conventional silver blade, but set into an iron base, identical to the Kephart rifle. Another feature that indicates the barrel is of later date.

New works in the triggers would pose no problems, since this feature was unchanged throughout. In fact, from the time of its first adoption until Gemmer dis-

PLATE NO. 43

Bottom view of the forearm of the Modena rifle, showing wear plate. Made of sheet iron, it is held in place by 14 small nails. Courtesy Colorado Historical Museum. Picture by J. D. Baird

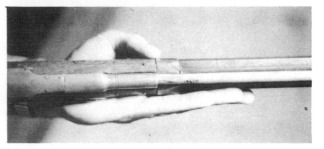

PLATE NO. 44

Lower thimble of Modena's rifle. Note two pins holding this fixture in place. Courtesy Colorado Historical Museum. Picture by J. D. Baird

continued making such rifles, the shape and function of the Hawken trigger remains unchanged, except for the decorative shape of the ends of the trigger bar.

The standard Hawken made lock of 1860 was too large to fit into the stock of the Modena rifle. Nor would the works fit into the existing plate. One of Adolphus Meier's locks would just clean up the old lock mortise, so the entire lock was replaced with a Meier lock, thus explaining an 1860 lock on an 1833 rifle.

The wear plate under the forend was examined carefully, with the thought that it might have been put on as a repair for a cracked forearm. Such is not the case, however, for its function is as described. It is retained in place with small nails around its circumference, 14 in all. Such a wear plate is not uncommon; a picture of Jim Baker shows that his Hawken rifle also had such a feature.

For those who are interested in statistics, we offer the following. The barrel measures 34 and 3/4 inches in length, and is of .58 caliber. The width across flats, both at the muzzle, and at the breech, is 1 and 3/16ths inches. The rifle weighs 12 1/2 lbs. The patchbox is of iron, the nine silver stars in the buttstock appear to be coin silver, and there is no engraving on the rifle. The lock is marked A. Meier, St. Louis, and Hanson speaks of Adolphus Meier as being listed as a dealer in guns and pistols in St. Louis in 1859. Meier used

PLATE NO. 45

Buttstock of the Modena rifle. Note iron patchbox and walnut stock. Courtesy Colorado Historical Museum. Picture by J. D. Baird

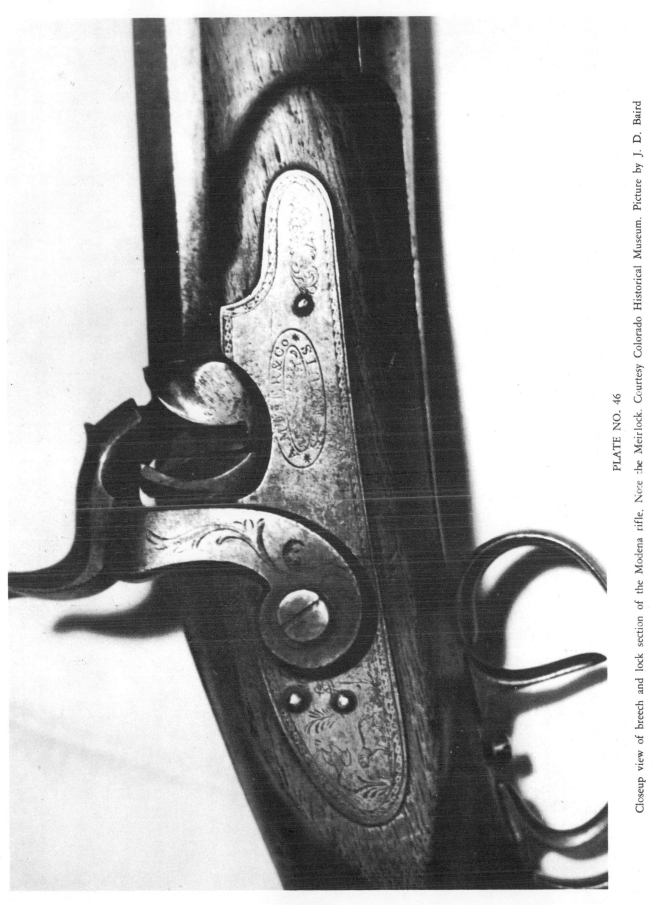

PLATE NO. 46

Closeup view of breech and lock section of the Modena rifle. Note the Meirlock. Courtesy Colorado Historical Museum. Picture by J. D. Baird

33

an oval trademark with, "A. Meier, St. Louis" and such a mark appears on the lock of Modena's rifle.

The coin silver lockbolt plate is of larger proportions than is generally found, and is held in place by two iron screws. It may be that this large plate hides the fact that in order to fit the new lock, the lock bolt had to be moved.

Found in the cheekpiece is an oval silver plate, inscribed with the following inscription.

Purchased St. Louis
1833
Mariano Modena
Gen. A. H. Jones
Big Thompson Colo.
1878

The barrel key escutcheons are of iron, inletted and held in place with screws. The barrel keys are not slotted for keeper pins. Ram-rod appears to be original, and the larger end is tipped with a brass ferrule, concaved upon the end, for seating the ball. The small end of the rod is fitted with an iron ferrule, drilled and tapped for a cleaning worm.

The forend tip is made of sheet iron, of rather difficult pattern. The rifle is stocked in straight grain walnut, with the grain running at an angle to the forearm. The buttplate is as has been described on other occasions, of sheet iron, hand welded construction. It measures 4 1/2 inches from toe to heel, and 1 and 1/4 inches across its widest point. The lock section tapers in thickness from 1 and 3/4 inches in front to 1 and 3/8 inches at the rear, and the wrist measures 1 3/4 inches up and down, 1 and 1/2 inches across.

Aside from showing much handling, the rifle seems in good sound condition. The stock has the usual number of scratches, nicks, and dents found in an old rifle that has seen much use.

It is these very nicks and dents that identify an old rifle as being just that; an old rifle. No matter how closely the craftsman comes to following every detail of a particular rifle, when making a Hawken replica, reproducing these fingerprints of antiquity is an impossibility. Those replica Hawkens being made today, no matter how accurate, will not pose any problem of identification to the serious Hawken student, as the modern made Kentucky rifles pose no problem to the expert in that field. Perhaps 50 or 100 years from now it will be difficult to tell the difference, but even that is doubtful.

CHAPTER 6

Engraved Hawken Rifles

By 1842, the firm of J. & S. Hawken was firmly entrenched in the western trade, with the reputation for making the best rifle obtainable for use on the plains and in the mountains. This "Rocky Mountain Rifle," as it was proudly called by the makers, Jacob and Samuel Hawken, had been used by the mountain men since Jake Hawken first opened a shop in St. Louis in 1815. Jake was joined by brother Sam in 1822, the same year Andrew Henry and William Ashley sent their expedition to the headwaters of the Missouri, in their revolutionary new concept of organized trapping expeditions.

Ashley liked Hawken rifles, had one made for himself, and you can be sure that out of the hundred men who made up that first contingent of "Ashley men," a number were carrying rifles with the new stamp "J&S Hawken, St. Louis."

As the Hawken shop recut, repaired, and supplied new rifles to these free trappers, their reputation for producers of fine rifles grew, wherever trappers met. More Hawken rifles reached the mountains in the caravans of trade goods that went up from the States each summer, to supply the rendezvous, and bring back the furs. Each year, as more and more traders and trappers took to the mountains, the need mounted for guns. Shotguns, pistols, and rifles, and all could be had by sending back an order with the returning caravan, to be brought up the following summer. For those who had lost their guns, traps, and other equipment, the caravans brought supplies of this nature, at double and triple St. Louis prices. Horsepacking such supplies long distances across the plains was a risky, hazardous business, but the potential profits were such that competition soon grew to such proportions that there was not enough business to go around. When the silk hat (or changes in the European economy—whichever school of thought one subscribes to) sent the price of beaver into a sudden slump, there was not enough profit to justify the risks, and the caravans no longer went to the mountains. Instead, the established trading companys built posts at advantageous points, preferably on navigable rivers, and supplied them by steamboat. The

trappers and Indians who wished to trade were forced to come into these trading posts, in order to dispose of their furs, and get new supplies.

While the price of beaver continued to slump, other furs remained in demand. Buffalo robes also enjoyed a brisk trade, and much effort was expended to get the Indians to bring their robes to the various posts. Mink, sable, martin, otter, even wolf pelts were traded for, with the trader offering tea, coffee, flour, sugar, powder and shot, knives, axes, blankets, beads, brass and sheet iron, brass buttons, awls, needles, and every knick-knack calculated to catch the eye of the savage. Often, when all else failed, whiskey was used for barter. Most of the trading posts were controlled from St. Louis, and the orders were, "Get the furs, at whatever cost." A drunken mob of Indians was a sickening, dangerous, soul-searing thing, but if it took whiskey to beat the competition, then whiskey was used.

From 1822 until such time as the Indian unrest made trade and travel in the mountains unprofitable, the fur trade flourished, supplying the Indian tribes with those goods of the white man they had come to rely upon, and acting as supply points for those hunters and trappers who still roamed the mountains. The emigrant trains came to be an important source of profit, and the shelves of the trading post carried every conceivable article imaginable—tobacco from Virginia, lead from the Illinois country, English, French and American gun powder, traps, guns, saddles, leather goods, blankets, endlessly the list goes on.

While Eastern gunmakers were busy supplying guns for this trade, the "ne plus ultra" of such guns were those from the shop of Jacob and Samuel Hawken. Having got their foot in the door early in the game, the Hawken brothers were careful that they did not lose the lead they had on all competition. They produced sturdy, compact, well made rifles for this trade, and a rifle marked Hawken, St. Louis, was always in demand, often bringing three times its St. Louis price, when sold off the shelf of the trading post.

Jacob and Samuel Hawken learned their trade in their father's shop in Hagerstown, Maryland. Christian

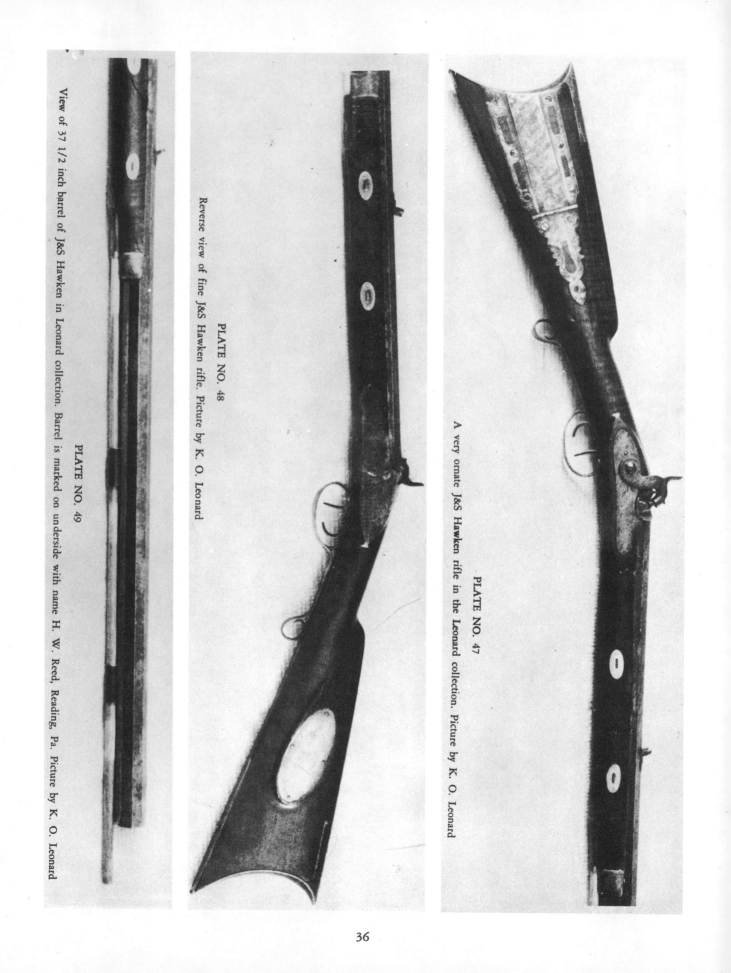

View of 37 1/2 inch barrel of J&S Hawken in Leonard collection. Barrel is marked on underside with name H. W. Reed, Reading, Pa. Picture by K. O. Leonard

PLATE NO. 49

Reverse view of fine J&S Hawken rifle. Picture by K. O. Leonard

PLATE NO. 48

A very ornate J&S Hawken rifle in the Leonard collection. Picture by K. O. Leonard

PLATE NO. 47

PLATE NO. 50

Rear sight of Leonard rifle. Sight is identical to one on Modena rifle. Picture by J. D. Baird

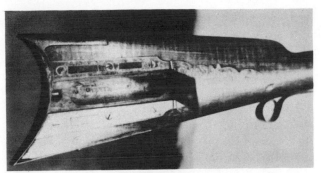

PLATE NO. 53

Patchbox lid in open position. Picture by J. D. Baird

PLATE NO. 51

View of breech. Note similarity between tang portion of breech and same area on Modena rifle. Picture by J. D. Baird

PLATE NO. 54

Engraved patchbox on J&S Hawken rifle in the May collection. Picture by Robert May

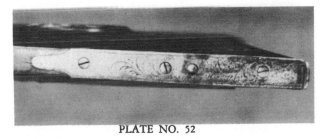

PLATE NO. 52

Engraved toeplate of Leonard rifle. Note patchbox lid release button in center of toeplate. Picture by J. D. Baird

PLATE NO. 55

Lock and breech of the J&S Hawken rifle in the May collection. Picture by Robert May

Hawken was a fine gunsmith, of the old school, and he taught his sons well. Jacob, the elder, worked with his father for a time, and there is at least one known example of their product. This, a typical flintlock, full-stocked Pennsylvania rifle, is marked C&J Hawken. The writer has examined one brass-mounted Pennsylvania rifle, with fullstock, marked C. Hawken in script, on the top barrel flat, midway between breech and rear sight.

That Jacob Hawken's training is apparent, can be seen when examining those rifles marked J&S Hawken. A straight edge on the upper comb line will reveal a slight hump; not a Roman nose form really, but enough of a hump to suggest that Jake's early training is showing through. Later S. Hawken rifles will not have this form; being a straight line from heel of butt to the point where the comb breaks over into the wrist.

The rifle pictured here is one of the most ornate Hawken rifles found, bearing the J&S Hawken stamp. One of the pieces in the Leonard collection, it has features not commonly found in any Hawken rifle. While it was made only a few years after the Modena rifle, it is considerably more ornate, although a number of construction features on the two rifles will be found to be very similar. We submit that the Modena rifle, when in its original state, had even more of the appearance of the rifle shown here.

Note the number of construction details that closely parallel each other—shape of scroll, outline of stock, shaping of lock section, cheekpiece, and sights. Particularly the rear sights, since these two rifles sport identical rear sights, of unusual configuration, and are the only two Hawken rifles yet examined to have this particular form.

Stocked in fine striped maple, other features of the rifle are typical of the work of Jacob Hawken in the 1835-45 period. The forend tip is cast in place, of pewter, the silver key escutcheons are nailed in place, and the rectangular-headed barrel keys are slotted for keeper pins. No such keeper pins were ever installed, however, thus suggesting that these small pieces of hardware were purchased from Eastern sources, as was the barrel.

This feature, of .56 caliber, 37 1/2 inches in length, is marked on the underside with the maker's name and address. Made by H. W. Reeds, of Reading, Pennsylvania, it is one of several Hawken rifles found with Eastern made barrels. This barrel is equipped with a hook breech, but the nipple is mounted in a brazed-on lug appendage, forming the breech. Note the similarity of the tang portion of this breech to that of the Modena rifle.

The engraving found on this rifle is that of Tristam Campbell, who is first listed as being in the Hawken shop by the city directories of 1842. Aside from the T. Campbell rifle in the Almquist collection, this is probably his most elaborate effort at decorating a mountain rifle.

The patchbox of this rifle is profusely engraved, as is the toeplate. It is in the toeplate that we find the button release for the patchbox lid, and the accompanying plates will show the function of this feature.

The double set triggers are of Hawken manufacture, but they are not double pull, in that the rear trigger must be set, before the front trigger will fire the rifle. They are, however, mounted on the long trigger bar, to which the scroll guard is also attached. These single-pull triggers are commonly found on the earlier Hawken rifles, and generally found on the lighter, much less expensive squirrel rifles made for the local trade.

The barrel for this rifle tapers, in that it is 1 1/16 inches across the flats at the muzzle, and 1 1/8 inches at the breech. Length of trigger pull is 14 inches from center of the buttplate to the front trigger, and the rifle weighs slightly over 10 1/2 pounds. The width of the lock section is 1 3/4 inches, both at the front and at the rear, not being tapered in this area as is common in later rifles. The buttplate is handmade of sheet iron, joined with brass, as has been described previously, and the front sight is the traditional silver blade in copper base.

The J&S Hawken marked rifles of the 1840's all suggest a trend toward a highly ornate form of decoration. Quite possibly the mountain men vied with one another as to who would have the most ornate rifle, and this rivalry is reflected in the existing specimens. At any rate, the contrast between these late J&S Hawken rifles and those rifles made by Samuel after Jake's death is almost startling. The S. Hawken rifle is nearly austere in its lack of decoration. As Boone once said of a companion's rifle, 'Its only beauty lies in its great power."

Robert May, of Chapman, Nebraska, has another J&S Hawken rifle that reflects the trend to a more ornate rifle. Mr. May's rifle is .55 caliber, with the barrel measuring 1 1/8 inches across the flats. The barrel is presently 28 inches long, but it has been shortened from the muzzle end. Original length was probably about 34 inches. It is stamped on the top flat, behind the rear sight, with the inscription J&S Hawken, St. Louis.

The patent, hooked breech and tang, toeplate, and patchbox are profusely engraved, again with the characteristics of workmanship attributed to Tristam Campbell. The side opening patchbox is rather unusual in shape, and is decorated with the likeness of a charging buffalo. The lid is opened by pressing a button located in the toeplate.

The lock of Mr. May's rifle is marked Wolfe and Bishop, Warranted. The hammer has been altered somewhat, possibly to facilitate carrying in a scabbard, or the rifle's removal from a gun cover. The patent breech is rather intricate, indicating that such work was not beyond the scope of the Hawken shop.

CHAPTER 7

Hoffman And Campbell, A Hawken Subsidiary

IT IS IN the city directories for 1842 that we first see the names of two men who are to play a bigger role in the Hawken story than any other employee. Christian Hoffman and Tristam Campbell are listed as being employed in the Hawken factory as journeyman gunsmiths. That they played an important role in the Hawken story is soon apparent, upon studying the city directories for the period.

In the 1845 directory, we find that Christian Hoffman and Tristam Campbell are listed as partners at 65 Locust Street. Of special interest is the fact that Jacob Hawken's son, Christopher M. Hawken, is also listed at this address. A study of the advertising material for that period shows a marked degree of similarity between that of the Hawken shop and that of the Hoffman and Campbell business, with only names and addresses differing.

Keeping in mind the throat-cutting business practices of the fur-traders during this period, and their efforts at cornering the fur trade, the boom town aspects of St. Louis, and the Hawken's past record of stubborn refusal to sell anything not made by them, one is able to make some reasonable assumptions. The demand for guns of all sorts was growing every day. Emigrants demanded rifles, less expensive than a Hawken, and the growing influx of Eastern sportsmen opened a market for a fancier rifle than the plain Hawken. The regular Hawken could not be considered a cheap rifle, selling as it did for around $30.00. A number of Eastern makers were offering plain rifles for as low as $7.50 each. Eastern sportsmen, while they might want a St. Louis made rifle, would be perfectly willing to pay extra for embellishments not found on the regular Hawken. Silver bands in the breech, checkering of the wrist, engraved hardware, and perhaps a fancy patchbox was about all that could be done to dress up a Hawken.

In short, a speciality market was developing, and the Hawken brothers took steps to get whatever part of it they could. One step would be to set up a different organization, under a different name, but staffed by trusted men, to handle those items in demand, but not handled by the Hawken store. Imported Eastern rifles, Colt revolvers, Allen pistols, and other such merchandise was selling readily, and through such an organization as Hoffman and Campbell, the Hawken partnership would receive a share of this business. Since Campbell was an engraver, he was perfectly capable of putting whatever was needed in the way of embellishments on a Hawken rifle to make it into a luxury piece. Anyone wanting an engraved Hawken at that time was probably forced to buy through Hoffman and Campbell.

The rifle illustrated here is an unusually interesting piece, in light of the above mentioned facts. Recently acquired by T. K. Dawson, it is marked Hoffman and Campbell, St. Louis, and is a perfect example of the J. & S. Hawken product of the 1840's. Stocked in walnut, with light checkering on the wrist, two silver bands in the breech, engraved iron hardware, it is typical of those rifles embellished by Campbell. Except for the unusally long barrel and absence of patchbox, it is nearly identical to the stock on the Mariano Modena rifle.

Although complete documentary evidence does not exist, there is a very good probability that this is the rifle of the historian Francis Parkman. Parkman loosely describes his rifle at various places in his book, *"Oregon Trail."* It is significant that at no time does he call it a Hawken, but refers to it as a St. Louis rifle. The unusual length of barrel, stock, and lock repairs, and area of its discovery all tend to give credence to the supposition that this was indeed the rifle carried by Parkman.

The rifle in question is very well preserved. The lock is marked Ashmore, the forend tip is of cast pewter, and the front sight is the conventional silver blade in a copper base. The silver barrel key escutcheons are nailed on, in lieu of screws, and the heel of the buttplate has been worn away, showing clearly the brass used to weld the top piece to the crescent. The cheekpiece is of beaver tail shape, but much smaller than later rifles, being very like that of Modena's rifle. The silver plate in the cheekpiece is uninscribed, and

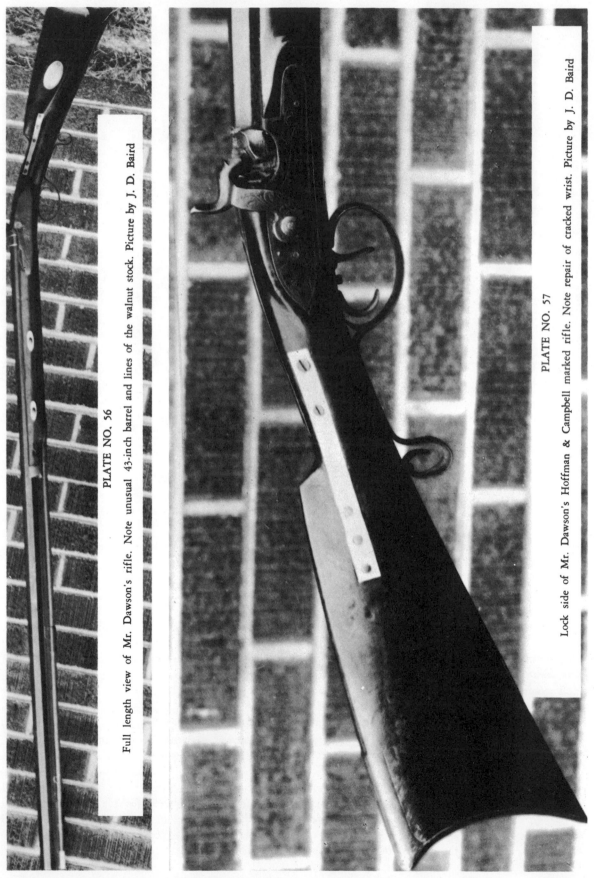

PLATE NO. 56

Full length view of Mr. Dawson's rifle. Note unusual 43-inch barrel and lines of the walnut stock. Picture by J. D. Baird

PLATE NO. 57

Lock side of Mr. Dawson's Hoffman & Campbell marked rifle. Note repair of cracked wrist. Picture by J. D. Baird

PLATE NO. 58

Close shot of Ashmore lock on rifle being discussed. Top, front edge of patent breech has been broken away. Note also that hammer screw is repaired. Picture by J. D. Baird

is held in place by two silver nails. The stock is straight grain walnut. Due to the 43 inch barrel, the rifle weighs nearly 15 pounds.

The interior of the barrel was remarkable in its state of preservation. Lands and grooves sharp, and unpitted, with just a trace of crud to be removed. What first appeared to be a slight funneling of the muzzle developed to be quite something else. The barrel was unbreeched, and a thorough cleaning performed. Lands are cut with a radius on top, seven lands and grooves, with one turn in 48 inches.

The interior form of the Hawken rifle barrel is the reason for the rifle's legendary accuracy. On the rifle in question, some very important questions were answered. Of .50 caliber, the bore is a slight taper from the breech to a point about 9 1/2 inches from the muzzle. Here a choke is apparent for about 8 inches, then from there to the muzzle, a slight flaring is seen. Measuring approximately .0005, about 1/4 inch from the end of the barrel, this flare suddenly increases an additional .002, giving the impression of slight funneling from rod wear. Close inspection has revealed that this is not the case, and that this is a deliberate relieving of the muzzle, in an effort to reduce rod wear, and more important, ease the starting of the patch and ball. The patched ball and rod are well into the barrel before resistance from the choke is felt thereby reducing the danger of breaking a ram-rod while putting down the ball. In a country where suitable wood for ram-rods is not available, such a feature would be most desirable. That it did not contribute to poor accuracy was readily apparent upon further investigation of the rifle's potential.

It proved impossible to resist the urge to test an original Hawken rifle, a la Kephart style. A proof load of 180 grains of 2ff powder was fired as a precaution, this being considered a double charge. Approximately fifteen shots were fired prior to the actual test, to ascertain if any defects were present. The morning chosen for the test was not ideal, but the quartering moderate breeze did serve as a comparison against conditions found on the prairie. A number of groups were fired off cross sticks at fifty yards, using the NMLRA regulation 6-bull 25 and 50-yard targets. Dupont 2ff powder was used throughout, as was Remington No. 12 caps. Notable was the complete lack of miss-fires, or hangfires. To my knowledge, the rifle has never failed to give fast and perfect ignition each and every time. During the test, the rifle was wiped between shots. Ball size was .495, and bedticking with lubricated bear oil served as patching.

Four powder charges were tried, with no effort being to correct for windage or elevation. The groups were fired purely to see how the rifle would place its shots, while using a six o'clock hold, regardless of powder charge.

The first group fired used a charge of 70 grains of powder. The center of the group was one inch below the center of the X ring. Group size was two inches.

The second group fired used 90 grains of powder, and the center of the group moved up about an inch and about half an inch to the left. While all shots were in the black, it was not much better than that fired with 70 grains.

Another 5 shot group was fired, this time using 110 grains of powder. Again the group rose a bit on the target, but began to tighten up. Number 5 was a flyer, approximately 3/5ths of an inch below the other four.

Again the powder charge was increased, this time to 130 grains, and this time things began to look good. The first four shots all went into a nice tight group, but unfortunately No. 5 fell out below about 1/2 an inch. Another 5 shot group was fired, using this charge, and this time all five shots went into a neat little group. Two more 5-shot strings were fired with this charge, and each time, the results were the same.

During a lull in the shooting, when the target was being examined, one very important thing became apparent. Those groups fired with 90 grains, 110 grains, and 130 grains were all in the black. Measurements later showed them to be in an area of less than two square inches. Adding in the shots fired from the first group, using 70 grains of powder, this area was increased to one of two inches wide by 2 1/2 inches high, yet with a variation of powder charges of as much as 60 grains. This seemed hard to believe, since all previous experience with muzzle loaders had witnessed complete chaos on the target when charges were varied more than a few grains. Great pains had always been taken to insure that the rifle was charged exactly alike each time. Not so the Hawken, it seemed to shoot pretty good, regardless of the amount of powder comprising the charge. One could easily see that this would prove very beneficial when loading hurriedly in a brush with Indians, or when running buffalo.

Francis Parkman had reported using his rifle to kill an antelope, at a distance of 204 paces, so it was decided to shoot a 200 yard, five shot group to see how it would hold up at the longer ranges. Using an 8 inch bull, six o'clock hold, with a moderate breeze blowing over the shooter's right shoulder, the rifle put all five shots into an area 3 inches by 7 1/2 inches, centered 8 inches below the bull and slightly to the left. With the proper sight corrections, the rifle could be made to put all of its shots into an 8-inch bull at this distance.

Not having a chronograph, it was impossible to come up with accurate figures on velocities, although they appear to be impressive. By doing some judicious measuring, and figuring, it was possible to plot a trajectory of sorts, showing where the ball would strike, in relation to point of aim, on all the different ranges fired. They were:

    50   yards................................1 1/2 inches high
   100   yards................................1   inch high
   150   yards................................2   inches low
   200   yards................................8   inches low

In conclusion, one must agree that the rifle is everything a hunting rifle should be. Ignition is quick and sure, accuracy is excellent, range and penetration very good for a round ball, and the rifle is sturdy, well balanced, and neatly put together.

Composite group of 20 shots, using four different loadings. Shot with .50 caliber J&S Hawken rifle marked with Hoffman & Campbell, group was fired by T. K. Dawson on April 30, 1967. 50 yard rest—.495 ball with bedtick patch greased w/bear oil
    5 shots with 70 grains 2 ff powder
    5 shots with 90 grains 2 ff powder
    5 shots with 110 grains 2 ff powder
    5 shots with 103 grains 2 ff powder
    Horizontal dispersement 2 inches
    Vertical dispersement 2 3/4 inches
    Picture by J. D. Baird

50 YARDS

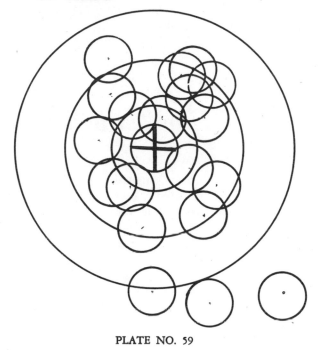

PLATE NO. 59

CHAPTER 8

Hawken Rifles For The Mountain Man

THE WRITER wishes to emphazise that the Hawken rifle was not a huge, clumsy, heavy club of a gun, as some descriptions would lead you to believe. To describe all Hawken rifles as weighing 12 or 15 pounds, firing a half ounce ball ahead of huge quantities of powder, is a little like saying that all horses have big feet and pull beer wagons. Certainly some Hawken rifles did weigh as much as 12 pounds, and some even weighed as much as 15 pounds, but these rifles were the exception, rather than the rule. These rifles were made up on special order, for and as very special purpose guns, for customers who wished the ultimate in long range accuracy and shocking power. Sometimes the customer wanted an extra long barrel, and this alone could increase the total weight of the rifle above the average. Some of the very heavy caliber rifles, such as Ashley's .68 caliber, was purposely made heavier throughout to give the rifle better balance and minimize recoil.

Double charging a rifle does increase the range somewhat, but it does so at the expense of accuracy. Double charging was resorted to more to increase velocity, thereby increasing energy, for close range, hard to kill targets like grizzly bear, and perhaps Indians.

To effectively increase range in a round ball rifle, you must increase ball weight, or size. A .64 caliber or .68 caliber rifle will shoot farther accurately than will a .40 caliber rifle, simply because the heavier ball will retain its velocity for a longer distance, and being heavier, will strike harder at long ranges. The wind will play havoc with a light ball, but the heavier ball will drift less, making possible longer shots under difficult situations. Such features would be most desirable to a buffalo hunter shooting from a stand, or a sea-otter hunter shooting from a windy beach. The Hawken rifles carried by the early trappers were not generally this large of bore, because they could not conveniently carry enough ammunition on their person to make such a rifle practical for an extended hunt.

Bear in mind, also, that to properly utilize the added ball weight of the large calibers, the powder charge must be increased proportionately. Heavy loads in a light rifle are not conductive to good shooting, because

recoil becomes an important factor. Increasing the weight of the rifle to help minimize recoil solves one problem and creates another. Increasing the weight of the rifle would add to the burden carried by the hunter, already loaded down with powder horn, pouch, knives, pistols, and those other articles he preferred to carry on his person.

Most Hawken rifles weighed in the neighborhood of 10 1/2 pounds, be it full stocked, or halfstocked. The halfstock's rib and thimbles does not appreciably reduce the weight of the rifle, but it does render this part of the rifle less liable to breakage. Something very important when you are many months from the nearest source of repair. The rifle weighed this amount, and fired a .50 or .53 caliber ball for some very important reasons.

Men went to the mountains for many reasons, and among their ranks could be found every form of human nature known to man. Good men, bad men, cowardly men, thieves, wanderers, dreamers, adventure-seekers, strong men, weak men, men of vision, and men of business. Some of them succumbed to the hazards of the country through weakness or stupidity ,some from overwhelming odds, and others crept back to the safety of the settlements, unknown, and unsung. Those men who survived, good men or bad, did so because of their ability to adapt to the country, and the way of life it demanded. Those who survived those first years in the mountains served as mentors to those who came after. They learned to live off the country for extended periods of time, with a minium of equipment or supplies. They carried on their person everything absolutely essential for their self-preservation, and bothered themselves with nothing that was not necessary for this purpose. A 10 1/2 pound, .50 or .53 caliber rifle, with its attendant accoutrements, and a supply of ammunition, must have been just about all the load they cared to be burdened with. At least, about all of their rifles that are left for posterity fall into this category. The writer's own experience with a .58 caliber Hawken style rifle has left him with some very definite ideas in this regard. Drop forty or fifty .58 caliber balls in your pouch and see if you do not take on a

Rocky Mountain News

A Scripps-Howard Newspaper

Reg. U.S. Pat. Off.

Colorado's First Newspaper—Founded in 1859

108TH YEAR, NO. 364   Second class postage paid at Denver, Colorado. Published every morning by Denver Publishing Co.   DENVER, COLO. 80201, FRI., APRIL 21, 1967

PLATE NO. 60

The masthead of Colorado's oldest newspaper, *"Rocky Mountain News,"* This Denver newspaper made frequent reference to "Uncle Samuel" Hawken, and the rifle shop that he established in Denver. Reproduced courtesy *Rocky Mountain News*

sudden list. If not then, carry them for a few days and then see how good it feels to take off that pouch.

Perhaps the mountain man did not carry that large a supply of balls at one time. The writer has no information as to what was considered a reasonable supply of ammunition, but under the circumstances, he thinks it would be all that could be comfortably car ried, and then just a little more, in case of separation from the pack animals. Disaster has a habit of slipping up on you when you are least prepared for it. The ones who lasted longest in the mountains were resourceful, wary, and took considerable care for im portant details. Keeping those things about you that could not be easily replaced would be only a common safeguard.

Because of his experience with a .58 caliber rifle to sharpen his comprehension, the writer noticed, while studying Modena's equipment, that the shoulder strap on his hunting pouch was at least four inches wide. A very wide shoulder strap would more evenly distribute the load from a heavy pouch, a feature you are quick to appreciate after a short time with a heavy pouch on a narrow strap. It would seem that the mountain man carried a heavy load, and used every device possible to make it more comfortable, but a heavy load, none the less.

This may be a good place to point out that a pound of lead will produce about 32 balls of .53 caliber, or approximately 40 balls of .50 caliber. A large horn, of the type carried by the mountain trapper, would hold nearly a pound and a half of powder. With an average charge of 100 grains of powder per shot, and even allowing generously for lead recovery, it still would be necessary for the hunter to carry nearly a hundred balls to properly utilize his powder. Ammunition would, of course, also be carried upon the pack animals, but we speak here of what he would carry on his person. There would be no need to carry more balls than he would have powder to fire, nor would he carry more powder than needed to furnish a charge for those balls he was able to carry in his pouch.

Here then seems to be the crux of the matter. The need for an ample supply of ammunition, balanced by the need for bullet weight and heavy charges, and its attendant weight problem led to a compromise. The early .50 caliber Hawken rifles fit this compromise most admirably, and later, as supply problems diminished, and ranges became somewhat extended, the .53 caliber came into the forefront.

It has been reported that one pound canisters of powder were favored by the mountain men, and this writer feels that the reason for this was their simple convenience. Weather proof, easy to pack, and as the powder was used, the amount of container would diminish, making the packing chore even more simple. A keg of powder, even a small one, would be a cumbersome thing at best, and would continue so until completely empty. Suitable for a hunting party working out of wagons, or as part of the supplies in a fort, but on the trail, or on the beaver streams, the one pound can was the thing.

It should also be understood that just because Horace Kephart tested his Hawken rifle with 164 and 205 grains of powder, it does not mean that the mountain man consistently charged his rifle with this much powder. It was meant to show that the Hawken rifle was strong enough to stand this double charging, and such a charge could be fired off the shoulder without too much shaking up. A bit of thinking will convince most of us that with powder selling for a dollar a pint, and the nearest source of supply over a thousand miles away, the mountain man, whether he carried a Hawken rifle, or a J. Henry, a Golcher, or even a Hudson Bay fusil, charged his piece with just enough powder to give acceptable accuracy and range. In the case of a .50 or .53 caliber Hawken, this would be between 80 and 120 grains of powder, depending upon the individual rifle, and its owner's ideas of acceptable accuracy and range. Horace Kephart, in an article on Hawken rifles in the April 15, 1924 issue of The American Rifleman, stated that the regular charge for a .53 caliber Hawken was 90 grains of 2ff powder.

45

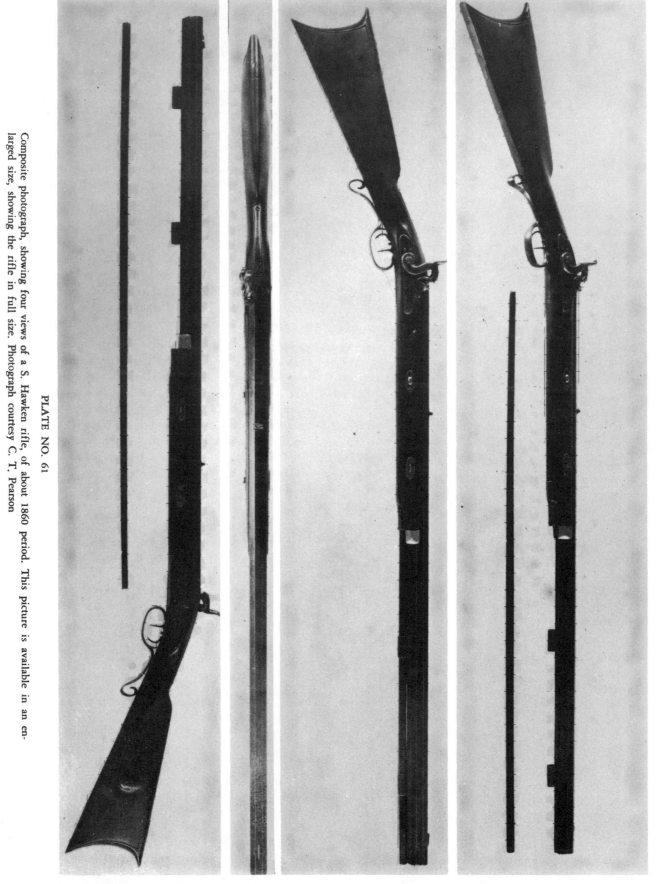

PLATE NO. 61

Composite photograph, showing four views of a S. Hawken rifle, of about 1860 period. This picture is available in an enlarged size, showing the rifle in full size. Photograph courtesy C. T. Pearson

46

PLATE NO. 62

Close-up view of the patent breech of an S. Hawken rifle of about 1860-65 period. Original shape of lock panel has been altered by injudicious sanding. Note rolled edge of upper part of lock. Picture by J. D. Baird

PLATE NO. 63

Muzzle end of barrel of the rifle shown in plate no. 62, showing front sight detail. Note use of iron base, a feature frequently found on the late rifles. Picture by J. D. Baird

My own rifle, of .50 caliber, gives great power, accuracy and penetration at 150 yards, with a charge of 100 grains of 2ff.

Nothing in these statements is meant to imply that the mountain man scrimped on powder. Indeed not, since powder was cheaper than hair, and these men were both practical and self-reliant. They simply knew from long experience, or quickly learned, what was needed, and the resultant demands they made upon the gunsmiths brought about a pronounced change in the style of rifles being built for their use. A sturdy, accurate, well built rifle of a weight both comfortable to carry, and to shoot, and using a ball large enough and at a velocity sufficient to do the job at hand was needed. The .50 caliber, 10 1/2 pound Hawken rifle filled this need to perfection, and in so doing, attained a very special place in the heart of every mountain man.

CHAPTER 9

The Slant-Breech Hawken

AFTER JACOB Hawken's death in 1849, Samuel was nearly overwhelmed with work. The year 1849 was a dilly for the Hawken shop, as it must have been for St. Louis as a whole. Jacob Hawken dead, Christopher Hawken gone, the Hoffman & Campbell enterprise wiped out by fire, and Samuel left weak from sickness and shock. It undoubtedly took a major effort on Sam's part to salvage what was left, reorganize and get back into production. The situation could not have been anything but chaotic in a city saddened by an unusually severe cholera epidemic, crippled by a disastrous fire on the riverfront business area, and then flooded by an influx of frenzied gold seekers hurrying through on their way West.

While Hoffman & Campbell were listed as being in business at 64 Locust Street, at least one city directory listed Tristam Campbell as still being connected with the Hawken business on Washington. Assuredly Tristam Campbell was available to help Samuel Hawken pick up the pieces, as was Sam's son, William S. Hawken. Whether Christian Hoffman came back to work in the Hawken shop or not we are not prepared to say, but we do know that when Jacob Hawken's son Christopher came back from the West, he and Hoffman opened a livery business at 13 & 14 Market Street, and were listed in the 1854 directory to that effect.

In this same directory, Sam and Tristam Campbell are listed as partners and advertising as Hawken & Campbell, 37 Washington. William S. Hawken is also listed in the directory as being at that address.

A discerning study of rifles produced in the early 1850's would indicate that Hawken quality had slipped somewhat. A rather distinctive change of style, plus a number of variants in construction detail all tend to show that the Hawken shop was hard pressed to meet the demand for rifles. The growing flood of gold seekers, home seekers, adventurers, and hunters flocking westward were demanding guns. While the trapper and Mountain Man was fading from the scene, his place was fast being filled by a new type of customer.

These new customers were not as discerning as had been the Mountain Man, but were apt to look more to price than to quality. One thing they all had in common—they were all in a hurry, and if Sam could not supply them with guns, they would look elsewhere. Quantities of eastern made rifles were being shipped to t. Louis with this demand in view, giving the Hawken shop stiff competition price-wise. The quality of Hawken rifles of this period reflects the tremendous pressures of the times.

While not necessarily one of the rifles made during this hectic period, the rifle pictured in plates 64, 65, 66, and 67 was certainly produced in the 1850-60 era. One of the rifles in the Leonard collection, it is unique in several ways.

Stocked in tiger stripe maple, the cheekpiece is a variation such as was discussed in another chapter. The panelling around the bottom edge is very similiar to that found on the Tristam Campbell rifle in the Almquist collection. This writer is inclined to believe that both rifles were stocked by the same person. Not often is such finely grained maple found on a Hawken rifle. A black and white picture can scarcely do justice to the varigated colors of yellow, brown and black.

Another unusual aspect of this particular rifle is the use of a cap-box. Of rather small proportions, and constructed of iron, it is rather interesting due to the scarcity of Hawken rifles so equipped. Our files indicate that a number of J. & S. Hawken rifles were equipped with patch-boxes of various styles, but this is the only Hawken so far examined that utilizes a cap-box. In fact, it is unusual to find any S. Hawken marked rifle with any such provision provided for either caps or patches.

In a preceeding chapter. we mentioned the cast metal buttplate of early pattern. The rifle depicted here is equipped with such a cast buttplate. While not quite as standardized in the use of castings as were still later Hawkens, nevertheless, this one shows features that were becoming commonplace on rifles of the late 1850's and throughout the 60's.

The forend tip is also a casting, and is held in place by a screw through the stock from under the barrel. Notes taken at the time of examination reveal that the scroll trigger guard is definitely of cast construction, but that the lower thimble is retained in place by the use of a single pin through the stock. The writer is inclined to believe that this rifle is of the middle 1850 period. However, one feature not found on any but late Hawekn rifles might tend to cause a reappraisal of this date.

We speak here of something not previously referred to, when describing Hawken rifles. The writer prefers to call this feature a "slant-breech" in that the rear face of the patent breech is not perpendicular to the line of bore. Indeed, this area is cut on a slant so as to cause the patent breech to measure 3/4 inches in length on its top side, and only 9/16 inches in length on the bottom side. The recoil face of the tang is also cut on such an angle as to exactly fit the slanting rear of the patent breech. Close examination of the joint between the patent breech and tang of the assembled rifle will reveal this parting as a line slanting to the rear of the rifle. Thus the reference to such a rifle as a "Slant-breech Hawken."

The major reason for such a fit-up was readily apparent to muzzle-loading barrel-maker William Large, of Ironton, Ohio. Bill was quick to point out the advantage of such an arrangement, when this writer expressed some question about it. In making a patent, hooked breech, one of the more difficult tasks is getting a good tight fit between hook of the breech and the socket of the tang. Putting this joint on a slant would make it much easier to make the cuts in the tang that allow the hook to slide into place, yet prevent any forward movement of the barrel.

While this arrangement definitely had its advantages, it is apparently a rather late development. Only a few other rifles are known by this writer to have this feature. One such example is the S. Hawken rifle once owned by Jim Bridger, and is now on display at the Montana State Historical Museum, at Helena.

Edward White, of Eldorado, Illinois, had the loan of another "Slant-breech" Hawken, and has used it to good advantage as a pattern for his efforts at duplicating the Hawken rifle. A cabinet maker and part-time gunsmith, Ed White has paid close attention to detail, and is really doing some fine work in reproducing the Rocky Mountain rifle. A wooden model he has made of the slanting breech and tang is as near perfection as anyone could ask for.

One thing in common all these "Slant-breech" Hawken rifles have are the features that definitely date them as being of late manufacture. Milling cuts on the face of the breech, among other things, are indications that machine tools were coming into use at the Hawken shop, during the late 1850's. Let us keep in mind that by then, railroads were operating between St. Louis, Cincinnati, and Pittsburgh, and thereby all eastern

PLATE NO. 64

View of buttstock and lock area of the fine, late, S. Hawken marked rifle in the Leonard collection. Picture by J. D. Baird

49

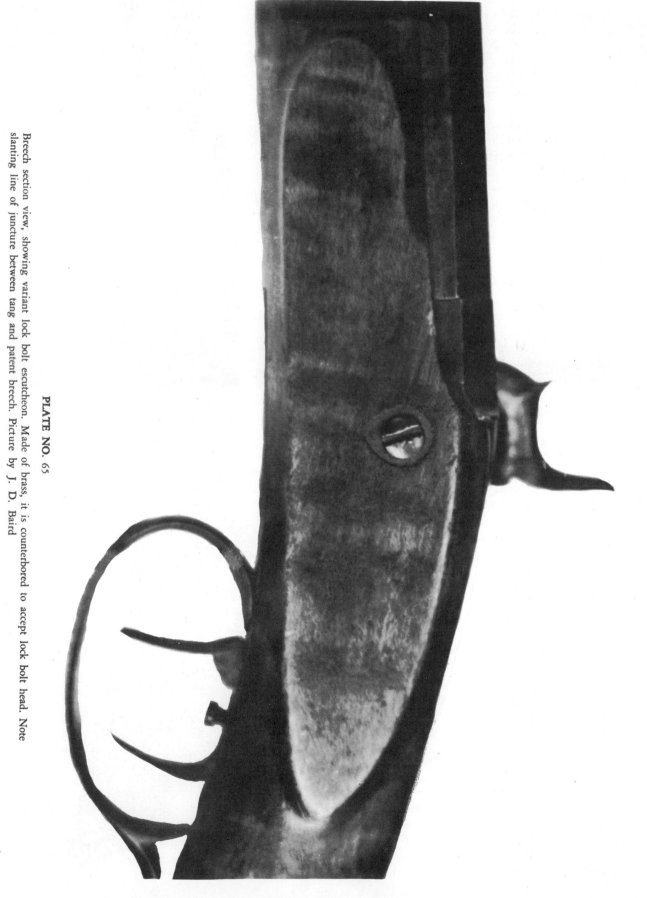

PLATE NO. 65

Breech section view, showing variant lock bolt escutcheon. Made of brass, it is counterbored to accept lock bolt head. Note slanting line of juncture between tang and patent breech. Picture by J. D. Baird

PLATE NO. 66

Close view of iron capbox on Leonard Hawken rifle. Note also that buttplate is casting of early pattern handmade buttplate. Picture by J. D. Baird

sources of supply. Henceforth, distance would be no barrier to technology.

It is the writer's opinion that the rifle pictured here is of slightly earlier vintage than is the one belonging to Bridger. Since Pierre Chien is supposed to have bought the rifle from Bridger in 1865, there cannot be over just a few years difference in their ages.

The rifle in Dr. Leonard's collection is of .50 caliber, with a 31 3/4 inch barrel that measures 1 inch both at the breech and at the muzzle. The barrel is stamped S. Hawken, St. Louis. The length of trigger pull is slightly shorter than is common, being only 12 1/2 inches from trigger to center of buttplate. As has been mentioned, the buttplate is a casting of early pattern, and measures 1 1/8 inches wide by 4 1/2 inches from toe to heel. The heel extension measures 3 inches and the toeplate is 5/8 inch wide by 3 3/4 inches long. While notes taken at the time do not reveal the exact weight of the rifle, they do record that it is noticeably lighter than most S. Hawkens of this class. Probably from the lighter barrel, and shorter buttstock, as it is a full inch shorter here than is most Hawken rifles.

Other notable features of the rifle being described here are very similiar to other S. Hawken rifles of this period. The front sight is the traditional silver blade, the escutcheons are of iron, and held in place by small screws. The trigger arrangement is double pull, in that the front trigger will fire the rifle as is, or will serve as a set trigger when the rear trigger is cocked.

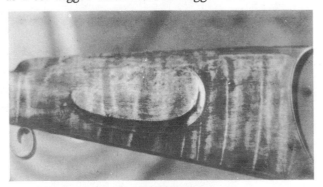

PLATE NO. 67

View of the cheekpiece side of the buttstock on **Dr.** Leonard's S. Hawken rifle. Note unusual shape of **cheek**-piece. Picture by J. D. Baird

51

PLATE NO. 68

The author examines a late S. Hawken rifle.

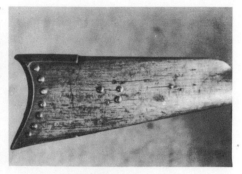

PLATE NO. 69

S. Hawken rifle in Leonard collection. Tacks are indication rifle probably belonged to an Indian at one time, but halfbreeds and even a few mountain men also decorated their rifles in such fashion. Picture by J. D. Baird

PLATE NO. 70

Kit Carson's Hawken rifle. Note cast buttplate of late pattern, and broad beavertail cheekpiece. Rifle uses the late "Slant-breech" feature described in text. Picture by C. T. Pearson

PLATE NO. 71

Another view of Carson rifle. Note sharp line of comb, where it drops into wrist area. Picture by C .T. Pearson

While we did not remove the lockplate from this particular rifle, its outside appearance is very like that of the one we examined at the home of Ed White. The lock of this rifle is marked T. Gibbons on the inside surface, and it is believed that the lock of the rifle being discussed here is also by that maker. Construc-

tion features of the two rifles all indicated that they are of the same period.

Another late S. Hawken rifle in the Leonard collection apparently has been owned by an Indian at some period of its history. Of late manufacture, with cast buttplate and other late features, it is well studded with brass tacks, one of the favorite methods of ornamentation used by the Indians. Such tacks were part of the stock of the fur trading posts. Plate No. 69 illustrates the buttstock of this rifle.

Kit Carson's S. Hawken rifle, preserved in the Masonic Lodge, Santa Fe, New Mexico, is another rifle of this late period. Of .53 caliber, with barrel measuring 31 1/16 inches in length, and 1 1/16 inches across the flats, it also uses the "slant-breech" feature so often found on these late rifles. In Plate No. 70, the cast iron buttplate can be seen to good advantage. Plate No. 71 again shows this rifle, and we wish to direct the reader's attention to the sharp comb line, where it falls into the wrist area.

Plates 72, 73, and 74 all depict the "slant-breech" S. Hawken in the Ressel collection. This rifle is also stocked in fine curly maple, as is the Leonard rifle. Differing in only minor details, the two rifles were very probably made the same year.

Thomas Gibbons was a gunsmith and gunlock maker whose locks are frequently found on Hawken rifles made after 1859. Gibbons is listed in the St. Louis directories as a dealer in guns and pistols, located at 187 Franklin Avenue. In one of the 1879 directories, he is listed as a gunsmith at 1522 Franklin Avenue. Gibbons came to St. Louis in the late 1850's, and is thought to have worked in the Hawken shop for a time. He is best known for his ability in producing a fine lock, and his locks are found on rifles made by other St. Louis makers such as H. E. Dimmick.

Robert May, of Chapman, Nebraska, reports that he has a little halfstock rifle marked T. Gibbons, Cov. Ky., on both lock and set triggers. Undoubtedly the same person as our St. Louis Gibbons, the Covington, Kentucky, address provides an interesting clue as to the origin of Thomas Gibbons. Plate No. 75 is included in this chapter to illustrate the working parts of a lock by T. Gibbons. We are indebted to Curt T. Pearson for this illustration, as well as Plate No. 76 and No. 77.

PLATE NO. 72

Ed White, Eldorado, Illinois, holding a fine S. Hawken "Slantbreech" rifle from the Ressel collection. Note finely grained stock. Picture by J. D. Baird

PLATE NO. 73

Close view of "Slantbreech" feature of Ressel Hawken rifle. Note countersunk head of lock bolt. Picture by J. D. Baird

PLATE NO. 74

Buttstock and lock area of Mr. Ressel's fine S. Hawken rifle. Rifle is equipped with T. Gibbons marked lock. Picture by J. D. Baird

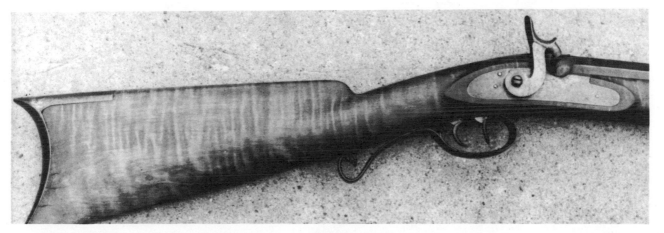

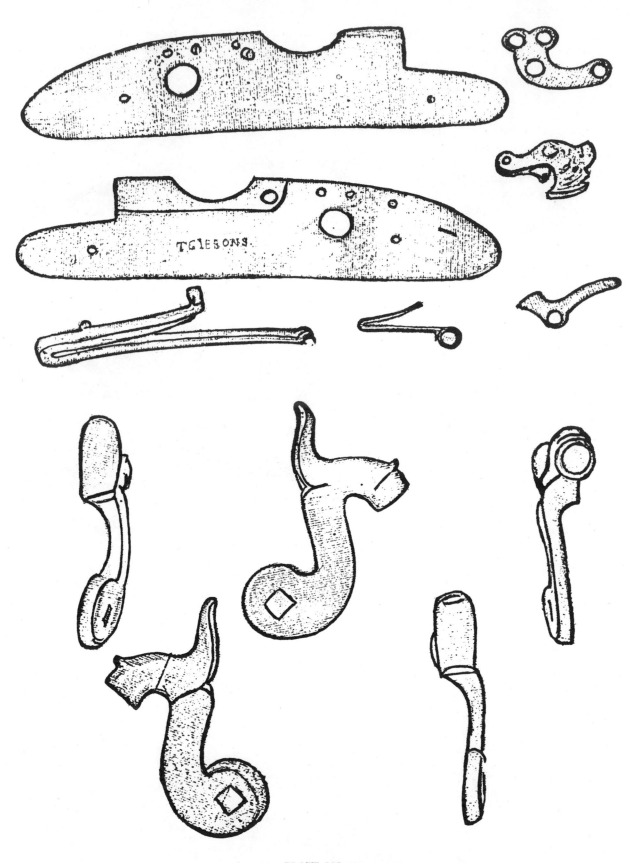

PLATE NO. 75

T. Gibbons percussion lock, after disassembly. Courtesy C. T. Pearson

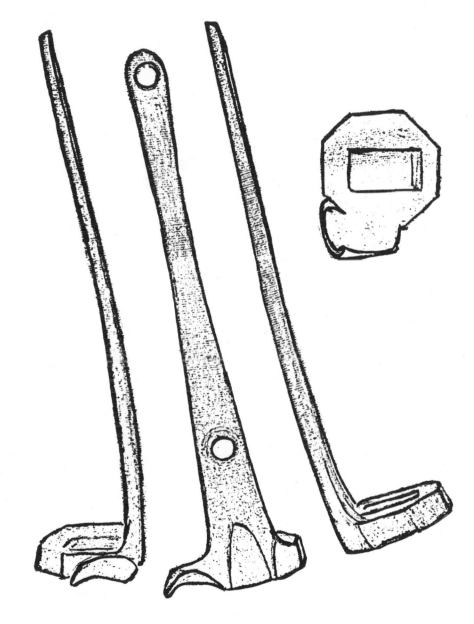

PLATE NO. 76

Four views of cast iron tang, used on late Hawken rifles. Courtesy C. T. Pearson

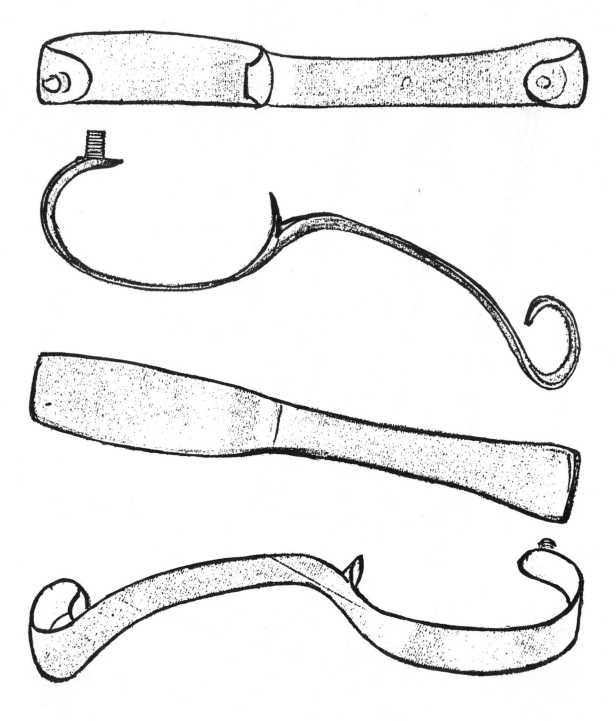

PLATE NO. 77

Four views of cast iron scroll guard as found on Kit Carson's Hawken rifle, as well as other late rifles from Hawken shop.
Courtesy C. T. Pearson

CHAPTER 10

Firearms Other Than "Mountain Rifles"

WHEN THE Hawken is mentioned, a great majority of those people acquainted with the name automatically think of the big bored, iron mounted rifle known as a "Mountain Rifle." It may come as a shock to some to learn that the "Mountain Rifle" was just part of the Hawken line of guns. That they formed the bulk of the Hawken production, did most to further the fame of the Hawken name, and are now the most sought after of St. Louis made guns will not be disputed here. Nevertheless, a complete line of firearms came out of the Hawken shop; including pistols, shotguns, target rifles and light rifles for the local trade. Some of their production (how much of it nobody will ever know) went to stock the shelves in hardware stores in St. Louis and elsewhere. That they did not always stamp their name on such guns has been well substantiated. Witness again the Kephart rifle, unmarked but later identified as a Hawken by one of the workmen who helped make it. Horace Kephart reported that he bought this rifle from the old Albright firm, and that it had been part of their stock. Kephart further stated that Albright told him that the Hawken firm would not put their stamp on a gun they made for another firm, if that company also made guns.

Some of the better, privately owned Hawken collections contain one or more Hawken marked guns that represent some of the Hawken production intended for different markets than that afforded by the mountain trade. While it is safe to say that most of their pistol production would meet the requirements of this mountain trade, as would their shotguns, some of the rifles produced in the Hawken shop clearly were meant for the local St. Louis trade.

In this latter category, there have been two distinct types of rifles preserved. The writer knows of several collections that contain one or more of the light caliber rifles made for the local trade. Generally of about .38 caliber, stocked in walnut or maple, iron mounted, or sometimes brass mounted, such guns are stamped S. Hawken, St. Louis, and are smaller, plainer editions of the larger Hawken "Mountain Rifle." Such rifles would serve very well to take the deer and turkey of Missouri, and the neighboring areas; were probably much cheaper to buy, and were certainly cheaper to shoot.

Another distinctive style of rifle produced by the Hawken shop for the local trade was what this writer, for want of a better name, has termed a turkey rifle. Those he has examined have been fullstocked in walnut, brass mounted, of heavy bore, and weighing in the neighborhood of 15 pounds. These rifles are big, with barrels as much as 48 inches in length, and generally around .56 caliber.

One such rifle that has been brought to the attention of the writer belongs to a gun enthusiast in Alaska. Marked J&S Hawken, the barrel measures 45 inches long, mountings are of brass, and total weight is 15 1/2 pounds. The owner reports that the rifle has the finest rear sight he has ever seen—must wear his best glasses to see to shoot it! Caliber is .54; it is equipped with patent, hooked breech, but lock is converted flintlock. While the writer does not have full information of this particular rifle, it appears that this may be a rather early specimen of the J&S Hawken firm.

The Leonard collection contains such a rifle, marked S. Hawken, and it is definitely of later manufacture. Of .565 caliber, with 48 inch barrel, the rifle weighs about 15 pounds.

The barrel is 1 1/8 inches across the flats both at the breech and at the muzzle, and is held in the walnut stock with three iron keys, as opposed to four brass keys found on the one in Alaska. The Leonard rifle does not have a patent, hooked breech, being equipped instead with solid bolster, with long tang, complete with clean out screw. The writer's Alaska correspondent reports that this rifle is also equipped with a clean out screw, installed at the factory before casehardening of the patent breech.

Both these rifles have a pinned on Kentucky style brass guard, and a Kentucky style double set triggers, but of larger proportions and more strongly built than was common for the Pennsylvania-Kentucky style rifle. Notes made at the time of examination of the Leonard owned rifle record that the rear sight is not standard

Hawken quality, but is of superior workmanship, with an extremely fine notch. Front sight is silver blade in copper base, in best Hawken tradition.

This writer would agree with his Alaska correspondent that both these rifles greatly resemble the product of Tennessee gunsmiths who specialized in the production of heavy rifles to be used in beef shoots and turkey matches. Thus the writer's inclination to refer to these rifles as turkey rifles.

Horse racing and shooting at a mark were two forms of amusement often indulged in at the distant trading posts, so it may be that some of these special Hawken target rifles were meant to sweep the field at whatever post the owner found himself.

The Leonard collection contains one of the light Hawken rifles made for the local trade. Stamped S. Hawken, St. Louis, and of .40 caliber, it utilizes one barrel key, a walnut stock, and a 30 inch barrel with solid bolster. No escutcheons were used, all mountings are of brass, and the forend tip is of pewter. The forend tip also forms the lower thimble, in that there is merely a hole in the pewter tip for the ramrod. While the rifle is unquestionably of Hawken manufacture, it does not reflect the workmanship one finds in the "Mountain Rifle" made by Jacob and Samuel Hawken. Such a rifle would serve very well for a homesteader, squatter or local hunter, and undoubtedly sold for considerably less than did the regular "Mountain Rifle." Needless to say, a "Mountain Rifle" would be somewhat in excess of actual need for the type of use it would receive in settled areas.

The William Almquist collection contains two specimens of these light Hawken rifles, as described above. Essentially they are the same as the one in the Leonard collection, differing in only minor details. The writer has heard reference to other such rifles being in private collections around the country, but unfortunately he has not been able to examine those rifles as of yet. In all probability the Hawken shop made a number of this type of rifle, most of which were unmarked, and disposed of them through such hardware outlets as Albright and others. Certainly the writer has seen several unmarked rifles that strongly smacked of Hawken workmanship, but unfortunately went away empty handed because he lacked information with which to make a positive identification.

Perhaps in the future, being armed with photographs, measurements, and a knowledge of what to look for, he will have better luck at seeking out these lost treasures.

The unmarked shotgun pictured here is the result of much searching for such a piece. Construction detail and characteristics of workmanship were sufficient to cause us to feel assured that it really was a long sought after Hawken shotgun. Unmarked with any name, as apparently is the case with all Hawken shotguns, nevertheless, to the practiced eye, it literally screamed Hawken! Even with the coat of grime and rust accumulated from years of hanging in an old barn, its authenticity was not doubted by those Hawken enthusiasts that examined it.

In the more leisurely atmosphere of the shop, some of the dust and rust was carefully wiped away, and a more thorough examination conducted. When the inside surface of the lockplates revealed the name T. Gibbons, the writer's exultation was complete. After spending a number of years searching for a Hawken shotgun, it would appear that the search was ended.

Charles Hanson, in his book "The Plains Rifle," dwelt with some length on the subject of shotguns and their use by trappers and hunters of the plains and mountains. Most of the better gunsmiths made shotguns, usually from parts obtained from sources in England and Belgium. That Hawken followed this practice is assured, since their advertising so plainly states that they were manufacturers of rifles and shotguns. That they did not place their name on such shotguns must be assumed, since there is no known specimen of such a marked shotgun existing.

J. P. Gemmer, who bought the Hawken shop and continued their line of guns, made both double barrel shotguns and shotgun-rifle combination guns, as well as a number of special purpose type guns. Double guns marked J. P. Gemmer are fairly common, but not to the extent that they can be found at just any gun show. The point we wish to make here is that if the Hawken shop had marked any of their shotguns with their name, surely at least one specimen would have come to light, in view of all the Hawken interest.

That shotguns found a ready use on the frontier has been well established. Henry Boller, Missouri River fur trader, whose letters and journal have been published under that same title by the State Historical Society of North Dakota, has frequent reference to the use of double shotguns. In one instance he goes to great length to describe in detail a light 20 gauge double gun he wished to have made and sent up to him at his trading post on the Upper Missouri.

Such accepted authorities as Parkman and Ruxton both allude to the use of such weapons, for defense, and for running buffalo as well. When the wagon trains started rolling over the Oregon Trail, in all probability a great number of shotguns were being carried along for use as pot guns, as well as for defense, should the need arise.

The J. & S. Hawken pistol illustrated in Plates No. 85, 86, and 87 is another fine piece from the Leonard collection. Typical of a great number of such pistols sold throughout the country, it may be viewed as evidence that the Hawken shop did indeed purchase such

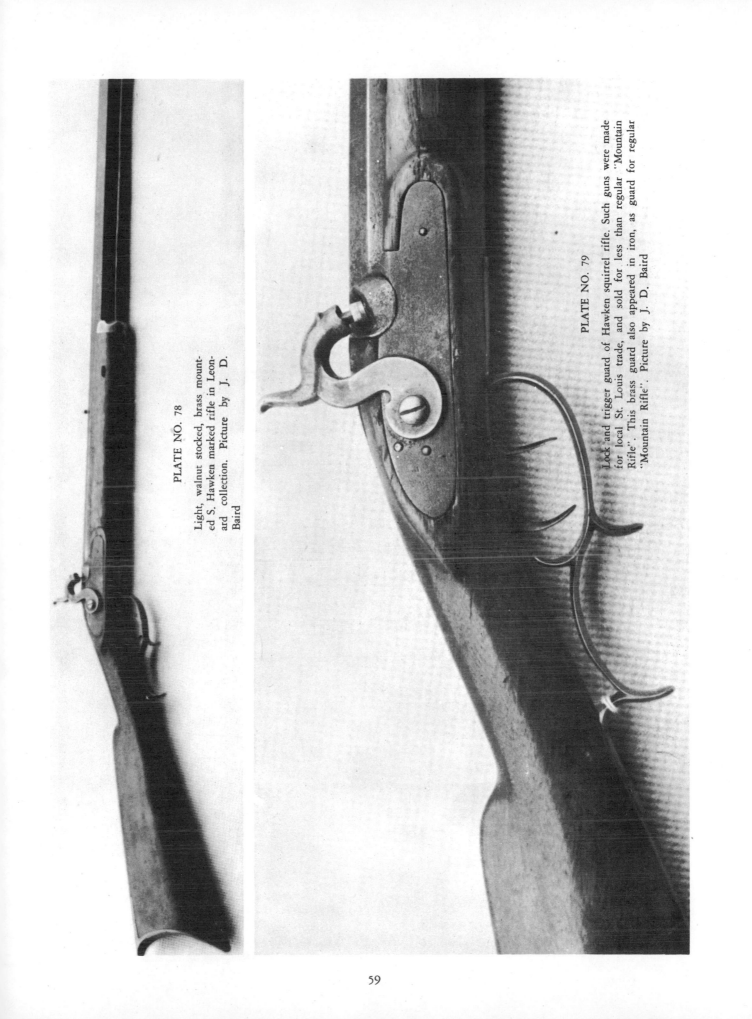

PLATE NO. 78

Light, walnut stocked, brass mounted S. Hawken marked rifle in Leonard collection. Picture by J. D. Baird

PLATE NO. 79

Lock and trigger guard of Hawken squirrel rifle. Such guns were made for local St. Louis trade, and sold for less than regular "Mountain Rifle". This brass guard also appeared in iron, as guard for regular "Mountain Rifle". Picture by J. D. Baird

PLATE NO. 81

J&S Hawen, 15 1/2 pounds, .54 caliber target rifle. Barrel length is 45 inches. Rifle owned by Harold Fuller, Cooper Landing, Alaska. Picture by Harold Fuller

PLATE NO. 82

Top view of barrel and breech of J&S Hawken target rifle owned by Mr. Fuller. Picture by Harold Fuller

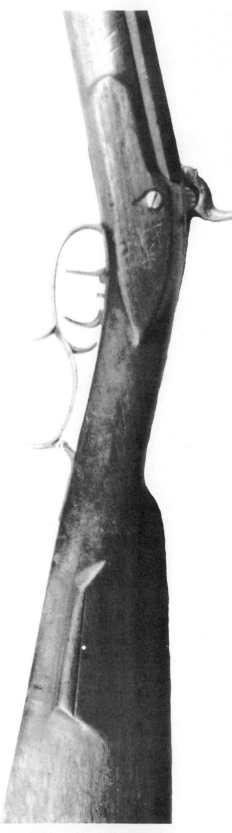

PLATE NO. 80

Dr. Leonard's S. Hawken squirrel rifle, showing Tennessee style cheekpiece. Picture by J. D. Baird

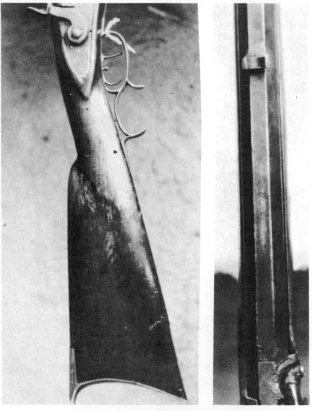

PLATE NO. 83

Heavy, walnut stocked, S. Hawken marked target rifle in Leonard collection. The writer has personally examined this rifle, and describes it in the text.

PLATE NO. 84

Top view of S. Hawken target rifle. Note cleanout screw in patent breech. Pictures by J. D. Baird

pistols for resale under their name. Witness the barrel stamping on the pistol in the Leonard collection. With the name J&S Hawkens stamped on the barrel, and the address St. Louis stamped on the back action lock, it undoubtedly was marked in that manner by the manufacturer. This could have been made at either the W. Chance & Co. or the Tryon & Co., both of whom furnished vast numbers of such pistols for the western trade.

Plates No. 88, 89, and 90 depict similar pistols, marked with names other than Hawken, showing the great similarity between such guns.

The two S. Hawken pistols in the Missouri Historical Museum of St. Louis were undoubtedly assembled in the Hawken shop, from components purchased elsewhere. The Hawken papers contain references to such components being purchased outside the shop. However, these pistols show unmistakable charactristics of workmanship common to the Hawken shop, as do the J&S Hawken marked pistols in the William Locke collection.

The S. Hawken marked pistols in the Missouri Historical Museum at St. Louis are very similiar to the above described pistol, but are equipped with bar action locks, instead of the back action lock found on Dr. Leonard's Hawken pistol.

All three of the Hawken pistols mentioned here are of the pocket variety, in that they were meant to be carried as an emergency weapon. Being of about .47 caliber, and using a comparatively light charge of powder, they would be too light to be of much use in running buffalo. In all probability, the occasion arose in which they were called upon to perform this service, but essentially they were meant to be a reserve weapon, to be used at close quarters, or if the rifle could not be brought into play.

Recently the writer's attention was directed to a picture of a pistol, one of several pictures serving to illustrate a chapter in a new book. Purported by the author to be an out and out fake, this pistol was stamped S. Hawken, and was a typical example of a cheap, very plainly made Kentucky style percussion pistol. The barrel was held to the stock with pins and a Golcher lock was used. The basis for condemning the piece as a fake was that the pistol did not meet the quality of workmanship found in Hawken rifles.

While this writer is in no position to question the judgement of those writers who examined the pistol in question, he would remind those who are quick to condemn a piece as a fake, that there is a very good book being published on variations in the 1851 Colt. The point in this is that a good many fine Colt revolvers have been pronounced fakes simply from lack of information. The writer's thought is that perhaps this may also be the case with other guns as well, simply

because they do not meet requirements of appearance imposed by limited information. Not many years ago, the fact of whether Hawken even made pistols was being hotly disputed. Those few in evidence now do not form a good basis of judgement on what a Hawken pistol must look like.

PLATE NO. 85

Pistol from Leonard collection, marked J & S Hawkens. St. Louis appears on back action lock. Pistol is believed to have been purchased by Hawken shop, for resale under their name, with engraving and silver work added by Tristam Campbell. Picture by J. D. Baird

PLATE NO. 86

Left side of Hawkens marked pistol. Guns stamped by Hawken shop did not use the name Hawkens—thus indicating this piece to have been made elsewhere for the Hawken brothers. Picture by J. D. Baird

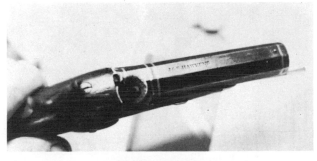

PLATE NO. 87

Top view of Dr. Leonard's J&S Hawken pistol. Pistol is rifled in about .47 caliber. Picture by J. D. Baird

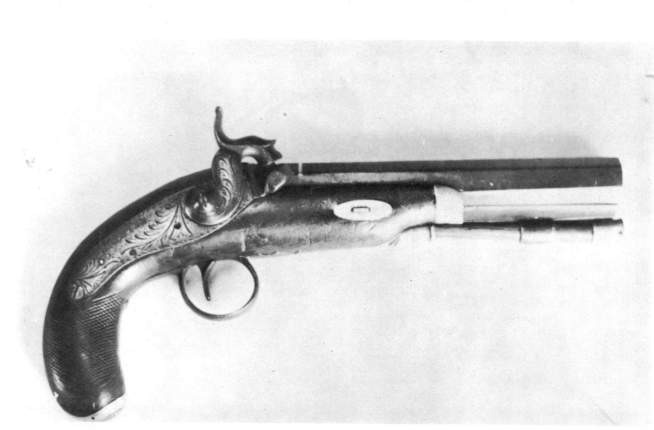

PLATE NO. 88

Percussion pistol of .47 caliber in Dawson collection. Typical of this type of belt pistol sold in vast quantities by Tyron & Co. and W. Chance & Co., as well as others. Picture by J. D. Baird

PLATE NO. 89

Left side view of Mr. Dawson's pistol. Such pistols were standard accessory in the Mountain Man's equipment. Picture by J. D. Baird

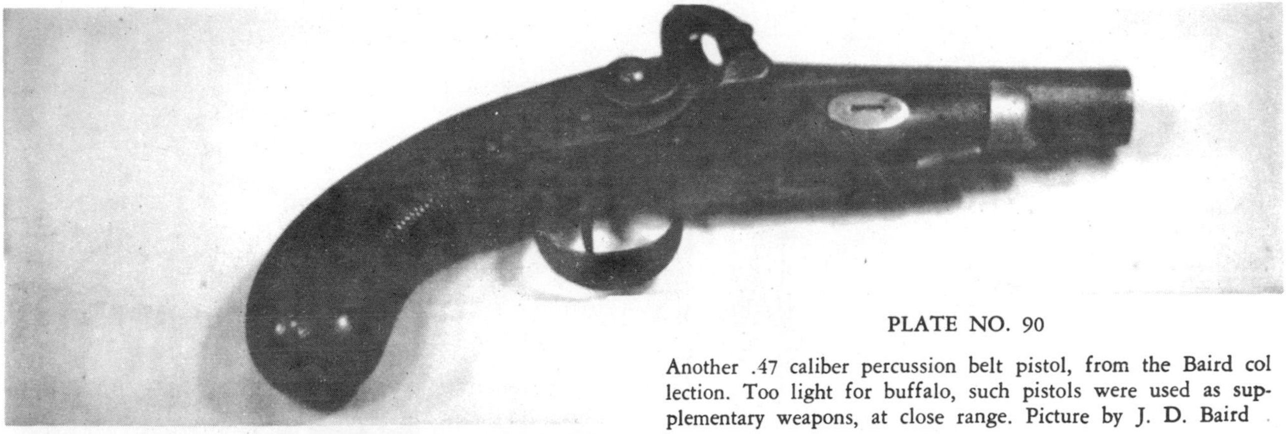

PLATE NO. 90

Another .47 caliber percussion belt pistol, from the Baird collection. Too light for buffalo, such pistols were used as supplementary weapons, at close range. Picture by J. D. Baird

PLATE NO. 91

A light, maple stocked, .38 caliber S. Hawken marked squirrel rifle from Wm. Almquist collection was fitted with variant iron scroll guard. Guard is identical to those found on H. E. Dimmick rifles. Picture by J. D. Baird

PLATE NO. 93

Terry Baird, son of author, holds his father's shotgun, believed to be unmarked Hawken. Picture by J. D. Baird

PLATE NO. 92

Nicely made rifle for local trade, this S. Hawken squirrel rifle from Almquist collection appears to use pistol thimble for lower ramrod thimble. Picture by J. D. Baird

PLATE NO. 94

Breech section of early shotgun, with all identifying characteristics of Hawken shop. Picture by J. D. Baird

PLATE NO. 95

Forend tip of S. Hawken squirrel rifle in Leonard collection. Note cast rear sight, and lack of rib for ramrod.

PLATE NO. 96

Fine J&S Hawken pistols in the Wm. Locke collection. These two pistols are excellent examples of the workmanship of J&S Hawken shop. Calibers .65, 10-1/8" octagon barrels stamped on top "St. Louis." Stamped on lock plates, "J. & S. Hawken." Iron trigger guards, half stocks, swivel type ramrods, German silver fore ends, wedge guards, butt caps and counter plates. Picture by Wm. Locke

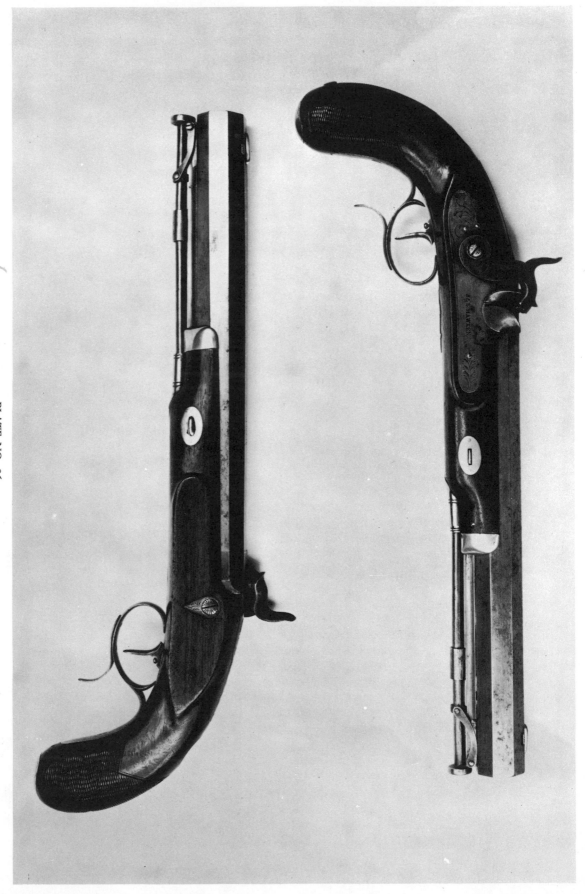

64

PLATE NO. 97

Variant cast iron trigger guard as found on S. Hawken rifle. From same mold as were brass guards sometimes found on Hawken squirrel rifles. From Leonard collection. Picture by J. D. Baird

In this line of thinking, we might point out that in 1835, Samuel Hawken recorded making a pistol for his son William. Since his son could not have been very old in 1835, it is hardly likely that Samuel would go to great efforts in building a pistol to quiet a young son's demands. A lock, a trigger, a barrel and a stock of sorts would comprise a quick solution to the insistent demands a young son can make on a busy father. While we do not suppose that the pistol alluded to in the book is this very pistol, we do submit that such a pistol as this would do very well in such a case as just described. It might be very well to lay such controversial pieces aside until such time as all doubt is removed as to their authenticity, before condemning them to a watery grave in the nearest river.

As a speculative observation, it may be pertinent to point out that the author has found, in those pistols examined, every form of patent breech found in the "Rocky Mountain Rifle," albeit on a smaller scale. All those craftsmen who have attempted to duplicate the Hawken rifle have remarked upon the difficulty they encounter when trying to reproduce the Hawken patent breech. Invariably they reach the conclusion that either the Hawken workmen were extremely dexterous with their primitive tools, or that they had access to more modern tools than is generally supposed. The writer would submit that the majority of these patent breeches were purchased in finished form, from eastern sources, and could easily have come from England, where the art of fine casting had long been established. These same craftsmen will agree with the sage observation that the Hawken workmen were much finer craftsmen than is generally realized, as will become apparent when their skill becomes the subject of attempted duplication.

CHAPTER 11

Spencer-Hawken Conversions

WITH THE ADVENT of War Between the States, firearms development advanced at a rapid pace. The most significant development in this direction was the invention of successful breech-loading, repeating rifles, firing the newly developed, fixed, metallic ammunition. The two most prominent names in connection with repeating arms used in this conflict were Christian M. Spencer and B. Tyler Henry.

B. Tyler Henry, in association with Oliver F. Winchester, developed a .44 caliber rimfire cartridge and a lever action, tubular magazine repeating rifle in which to fire it. The subsequent development of this cartridge and the Henry rifle is the well known Winchester story, often told in print and lately on the screen. We are more concerned here with what part Christian M. Spencer's famous rifle played in the Hawken story.

First patented in 1860, the Spencer rifle has the distinction of having been personally approved of as a military weapon by President Lincoln. While the military bought vast numbers of arms from any source they could be found, the Spencer was the main repeating rifle for this service. Before the conflict had ended, well over 70,000 Spencer rifles had been delivered to the Federal Government, along with some 60,000,000 rounds of the rimfire, copper cased ammunition. With the number of rifles in service, it is easy to understand that upon conclusion of the fighting, considerable numbers of these rifles would find their way into civilian usage.

As is usually the case with returning servicemen after the blood and thunder of war, the old homestead seemed rather tame. With the great expanse of an undeveloped West to serve as a lure, it is only natural that a great number of these ex-service men turned their faces westward to establish new homes, new hopes, and new roots. Spencer rifles went West with these emigrants, as did every other form of firearm then in use.

That the shooting public was well aware of the advantages of repeating arms could not be disputed. Either through personal experience, or hearing stories from ex-soldiers of the exploits in which the Spencer played a part would do much to further the public trend tow-

ard this type of firearm. The influx of these returned military Spencer rifles would only tend to speed up this trend. For normal use, such as the taking of game, and protection of the home and livestock, the Spencer would serve very well. Ease of loading, rapidity of fire, and the comfortable feeling inherent in a full magazine of cartridges would do much to make the Spencer popular with westward bound emigrants.

While later events were to show the need for better, more powerful arms, at the close of the War Between the States, the Spencer rifle was considered a very reliable, powerful gun, eminently suited for Western use. That J. P. Gemmer, St. Louis gunmaker and successor of the Hawkens, was in agreement with this commonly held opinion of the Spencer is testified to by the number of these rifles he sporterized in his shop. It would be difficult to determine whether such work was brought to the old Hawken factory by Spencer owners who valued the Hawken barrel, or was simply a method by which Gemmer could reach that ever-growing market provided by those who insisted on a breech-loader. Certainly by the late 1860's makers of muzzle-loading rifles could see the handwriting on the wall for their products. Of course, a few die-hard users could be heard proclaiming, "No puny breech-loader is ever going to replace my Hawken, (or Dimmick, or Lewis, or James, etc.) for buffalo or Injun!" To be sure, it would seem that a 40 grain charge in a breech-loader could never replace the 90 to 130 grain charge of a Hawken "Mountain Rifle". But these light loads were only a first step, caused by the limitations imposed by the thin copper cases used in rimfire ammunition for the Henry and the Spencer. With the development of center fire ammunition, with its strong, brass cases, heavy bullets and heavy charges, the big bored, muzzle-loading mountain rifles had, at last, met their match. When performance matched performance, rapidity of fire easily tipped the scales in favor of the "catridge" gun.

We speak here of a transitional period. An era of time immediately following the war, with firearms development going off in all directions. The Henry,

PLATE NO. 98

Hawken-Spencer conversion marked J. P. Gemmer St. Louis on top barrel flat. Forend bored full length for cleaning rod, equipped with cast iron forend tip, new trigger, rifle is best example of such sporterizing jobs performed in the Hawken shop. Photograph courtesy E. M. Louer

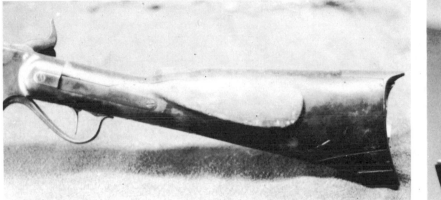

PLATE NO. 99

Cheekpiece view of buttstock of Hawken-Spencer in Louer collection. Note new trigger, and cast buttplate of later pattern.

PLATE NO. 100

View of buttplate of Hawken-Spencer in Louer collection. Magazine end has been reworked to fit in Hawken buttplate.

PLATE NO. 101

Forend of Hawken-Spencer conversion. Note excellent workmanship of J. P. Gemmer. Courtesy E. M. Louer

later to be known as the Winchester, was to develop a .44 caliber center-fire cartridge; while Sharps, another famous name is guns, was to rely completely upon their single-shot, but work feverishly toward developing bigger and longer ranged loads for it. Successful as they were in this endeavor, they held the lead only until the repeaters could duplicate their performance ballistically. But for a time, admittedly a short time, the Spencer was equal to the best rifles available, and far superior to most.

John Phillip Gemmer's ability as a gunsmith and businessman cannot be doubted. That he was able to assume control of the Hawken business, adapt it to the changing needs of the times, and continue it as a profitable business until the time of his retirement is sufficient proof of his ability. A young man, with young ideas, he was quick to see his need for a breech-loading rifle with which to capture his share of this rapidly

growing market. Taking the best features of the two top rifles of the times, and merging them into one gun would be a logical step. It is thus we have the Spencer-Hawken rifle.

Using the Spencer action, and the tubular magazine feature, Gemmer built rifles on the Hawken lines, but with the Spencer's firepower. There can be little question but what he had the use of some machine tools. Cuts in the barrel for extractor, threading of barrels, and making the magazine cut in the buttplate would be much simplified with the simplest of machine tools. Having served through the war as a gunsmith, with the rank of Corporal, in the Government Arsenal, Gemmer would have been prepared to make such alterations and adaptions.

A few gun collectors have been under the impression that these Spencer conversions were made simply by cutting surplus Hawken rifles in two and inserting the

Spencer breech. That such an idea is totally false can be demonstrated by comparing a few features of Hawken rifles vs. Spencer rifles.

The most important area is that of the wrist and tang. The Spencer is noticeably thicker here than in any Hawken, and a cut-off stock simply would not begin to fit. The inletting for the long Hawken tang, as well as for the Hawken guard would need be filled, even if the breech of a Spencer could somehow be worked down to fit a Hawken stock. How much easier it would be just to make a new buttstock, and this of course, was what happened. On the forearm, the treatment varied somewhat on different rifles examined. Usually the regular cast forend tip was used, but occasionally this feature was neglected. In most cases, the barrel had an under-rib, fitted with thimbles for a wiping stick, but on some of the rifles examined, this feature had been removed, and the hole in the forend plugged.

Another point in question—the regular Hawken barrel used a twist of 1 turn in 48 inches—hardly a suitable twist for the Spencer bullet, even if bore diameter happened to be correct. Much more likely is the premise that barrels were made especially with this conversion in mind. In short, this writer is adamant in his belief that the Spencer-Hawken was a new product of J. P. Gemmer, based on the Spencer action, but using new parts made in the shop for this purpose.

One point of variance with these Spencer conversions is the stamping on the barrel. The writer's Arizona correspondent reports that he has such a converted Spencer-Hawken, and it is stamped on the top barrel flat, J. P. Gemmer, St. Louis. Those examples examined by the writer have all been stamped S. Hawken, St. Louis. Keeping in mind Gemmer's deliberate intention of making these rifles continue the Hawken tradition, such a stamp can be easily understood. That he later made breech-loading single-shot rifles very nearly like the Hawken "Mountain Rifle," but stamped with the name J. P. Gemmer can only be taken as a reluctant admission on his part that the day of the percussion Hawken was fast drawing to a close. Even when such

guns were considered relics by a cartridge minded public, his refusal to part with one for less than regular price is further indication of the sentiment he attached to the Hawken "Mountain Rifles."

The Spencer-Hawken rifle pictured here is typical of that type rifle examined by the writer. Being part of the Leonard collection, it, unlike so many rifles examined over the years, does have a history connected with it. We shall attempt to tell that story as it was related to us.

The rifle's original owner, a young ex-soldier, was making his way to the Grasshopper Creek mines at Bannack, in what is now Montana. Along the way, he surprised and assaulted a little Indian girl, whose family was of a group gathering Awawsun's serviceberries. While he was in the act of attacking the little girl, the girl's brother who had heard her cry for help, slipped up and killed the assailant with a blow to the head with a rock. By virtue of the deed, the boy was allowed to keep the white man's weapons.

One of Mariano Modena's friends and occasional hunting partners was a man commonly called Livereating Johnson, whose name was gained from the gruesome act he performed upon every Crow Indian he killed in pursuance of an oath to exterminate them.

Johnson, being in the area, and learning of the rifle, heard from the Indian boy's family how he had acquired the rifle, and why he had been allowed to keep it. Since Johnson desired such a gun for himself, he took the first opportunity to attack the boy, killed him with a knife, and escaped with the rifle. His exultation must have been shortlived, for he found that it was not nearly as powerful as he had imagined, being at best, a close range weapon.

At some later date, while in Virginia City, Johnson traded this rifle to a Mr. Louis Romey, whose word was passed along concerning the circumstances surrounding the rifle. It is hard to understand in this day and age how such a ruthless murder of a boy for a mere rifle could be looked upon with indulgence, but we must remember such was the sentiment of the times. Indians were

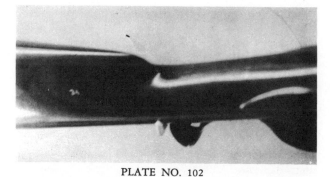

PLATE NO. 102

Detail view of comb area on fine Gemmer breechloading Hawken rifle in Missouri Historical Society Museum, St. Louis. Picture by J. D. Baird

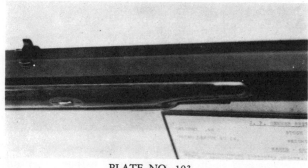

PLATE NO. 103

Detail view of rear sight and forend tip on Gemmer rifle in Missouri Historical Society Museum, St. Louis. Picture by J. D. Baird

considered worse than lice, their children nits, and it was no more wrong to kill the children than it was to kill the braves or the women. Such acts carried no penalty, but were awarded with praise and approbation. Livereating Johnson had the respect, the fear, and the hatred of the entire Crow nation.

While Johnson served in the War Between the States, one would wonder why he was not better acquainted with the potential of the Spencer rifle. Perhaps his long experience with, and respect for, the Hawken rifle led him into the mistaken belief that their name on the barrel would, in some manner, greatly increase the rifle's worth.

Any collector who wishes such a rifle today can wryly point out that while such an assumption might have been in error in Johnson's time, it is in error no longer. The Hawken name has indeed increased the worth of such a rifle. For that matter, the name of J. P. Gemmer has increased the worth of these rifles, for as the interest in Hawken grows, so grows the value of anything connected with their shop.

It may be well to emphasize one fact that is not generally known. With the development of the breech-loading rifle, it is true that muzzle-loading rifles became obsolete. However, until such time as the breech-loaders could equal the ballistic performance of the Hawken, they could not completely replace it. Indeed, it was not until well into the 1870's that firearms technology could produce any breech-loading gun even closely equalling ballistic performance of the Hawken.

Firepower—that rapidity of fire inherent in breech-loaders, was to be the biggest asset of the new rifles. Long range knockdown power was to remain the exclusive domain of Hawken, Dimmick, and other plains rifles of the period, that were capable of using heavy charges of powder. This domain was usurped by breech-loaders only after the development of the brass cartridge case, with its centrally located primer, made possible heavy charges behind long, heavy bullets that retained their velocity better than could the round ball of the muzzle-loader.

In that interim between first development of the metallic cartridge and its ultimate development into extremely powerful, long ranged loads, the rifleman was forced to make a choice. If sustained fire at moderate ranges was important, the new breech-loaders would serve admirably. Should the need demand a rifle capable of delivering a smashing blow at long range, the Hawken, or Dimmick and other muzzle-loading plains rifles, had to be resorted to.

CHAPTER 12

J. P. Gemmer, Successor To The Hawkens

THERE IS SOME conflict of opinion as to just how and when John Philip Gemmer acquired the Hawken business. His son, Julius P. H. Gemmer, who for many years, was connected with the Winchester Repeating Arms Company, is credited as the source that his father purchased the business from Samuel Hawken in October of 1862.

Horace Kephart, in an article written for the *American Rifleman* of April, 1924, stated that Gemmer told him he purchased the business from William L. Watt and Joseph Eterle in 1862. Horace Kephart's friendly relations with Gemmer and the employees of the old Hawken shop should assure that his information be as accurate as that of anyone.

It should be remembered that the actual circumstances of the transfer of ownership probably was not considered to be of earth-shaking consequence, so it is doubtful if anyone bothered to record every small detail. In view of the circumstances, one could be excused for indulging in a bit of speculation as to how and when the ownership actually changed hands. When one is faced with choosing between public records, and the record of events as recalled from memory, it is discretion that prompts us to rely upon the public record.

Using recorded facts, and supplementing these with an understanding of current events of the period, we can often make creditable assumptions as to what probably took place. Before we indulge in such an exercise, let us review the public record.

The St. Louis directories for the year 1859 listed William S. Hawken, son of Samuel, as being the proprietor of the Hawken business at 21 Washington Avenue. Since Samuel Hawken left the city on April 20th, he must have turned the shop over to his son in 1858, in order for the directory for 1859 to pick up the change of ownership. It is safe to assume that Samuel Hawken did not just pick up and go; such a trip would require advance planning.

The very next year the directories record another change in ownership of the Hawken business. Here again, we may assume that the change took place either late in 1859, or very early in 1860, so that the directories for that year could reflect the change. We do not mean that the timing was deliberate; just that the changes took place before the directories were made up for each particular year, and therefore could be reflected in those directories.

At any rate, the directory for 1860 shows the following advertisement.

William L. Watt
Successor to W. S. Hawken
Rifle & Shotgun Manufacturer
21 Washington Ave.
Hawken Rifles always on hand

Now here is a fine point! William Watt was advertising as always having Hawken rifles on hand. He does not say that he has S. Hawken rifles; simply that he has Hawken rifles on hand. He was perfectly aware that Samuel Hawken was in the gun manufacturing business in Denver, yet he is listed as being the proprietor of the business in St. Louis. Why advertise a change in proprietorship, if indeed, Samuel Hawken had merely taken a vacation of sorts, and left his shop in the hands of others? The only logical conclusion one can reach is that William L. Watt did indeed purchase the business, or at least a controlling interest, from William S. Hawken, who had received it from his father, or who was acting in his father's behalf. Upon completion of these negotiations, William S. Hawken went to Denver, Colorado Territory, to join his father. When Sam later decided to return to St. Louis in retirement, William S. took over management of the Denver shop.

It is interesting to speculate about how William L. Watt marked the rifles he made and sold while Samuel Hawken was in Denver. Did he simply make rifles in the Hawken style and leave them unmarked? One rifle has come to this writer's attention that could conceivably be a clue to this puzzle. This rifle, in the collection of Edwin Louer, of Tucson, Arizona, while undoubtedly of 1855-65 vintage, has as its only marking, the single word 'Hawken." While there is no doubt about the rifle's authenticity, it does reflect work-

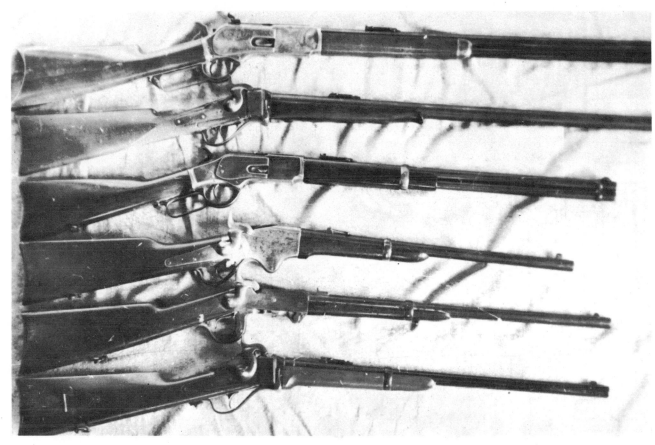

PLATE NO. 107

Sharps paper cartridge rifle, Burnside carbine, Spencer repeating rifle, 1873 Winchester 44-40 caliber, Sharps "business rifle" 45-70 caliber, 1876 Winchester, 45-75 caliber.

Beginning with the Sharps paper cartridge rifle, the Hawken shop was to feel the competition from the breech-loading rifles above. With the advent of such rifles as the heavy Sharps and the 76 Winchester, the demand for muzzle-loading rifles came to an end. Picture by J. D. Baird

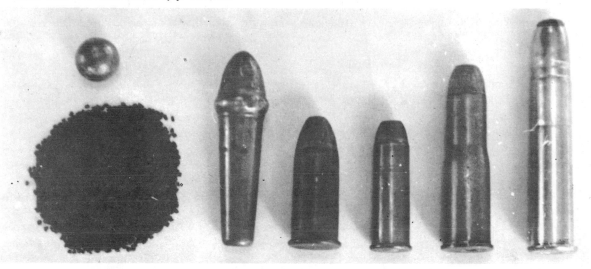

PLATE NO. 108

From left to right—
150 grain charge and .53 caliber ball for Hawken muzzle-loading rifle, .52 caliber Burnside carbine cartridge, .52 caliber Spencer rimfire cartridge, .44-40 Winchester centerfire cartridge, .45-75 Winchester centerfire cartridge, .45-70 Government centerfire cartridge.

Burnside, Spencer and 44-40 Winchester loads could not equal heavy load of Hawken rifle. The 45-70 Government and 45-75 Winchester surpassed the Hawken capabilities, and contributed to the demise of the muzzle-loading rifle as a serious hunting and defense weapon. Picture by J. D. Baid

71

manship a bit different than that encountered in other Hawken rifles. This writer is of the opinion that this is one of the rifles made and marketed by William Watt. His use of the name Hawken would be acceptable, since he had purchased the business, and the name was a recognized trademark. Because Sam was still making rifles and marking them S. Hawken, Watt probably was not free to use the full name. Gemmer, who came into ownership after Sam's retirement, was under no such restrictions. It may be that he negotiated an agreement with Samuel that would assure him unfettered use of the Hawken stamp. Gemmer, who had an interest in the shop, would have been quick to see the advantage of having unlimited use of the full Hawken stamp. We submit that this is the agreement negotiated between he and Samuel Hawken in 1862, and that the passing of time and faulty memories have contributed to the present day confusion about the various transfers of ownership.

The October 1940 issue of *Muzzle Blasts* carried an article copied from an issue of *"Arms Collector of the United States,"* and whose original author was Julius H. P. Gemmer, son of John Philip Gemmer. In this article, Julius Gemmer established the fact that his father was born in Nassau, Germany, in June of 1838. His parents were William and Maria Gemmer. After his mother passed away, John P. Gemmer accompanied his father to the United States in 1855, crossing the Atlantic in a sailing ship, and landing in New Orleans. After traveling up the Mississippi River by steamboat, the Gemmers located in Booneville, Missouri, and remained there for four years. It is here that J. P. Gemmer first learned the gunsmithing trade, but it is not known for whom he served as apprentice while in Booneville.

The year Samuel Hawken went to Denver, Gemmer arrived in St. Louis and found employment with Emanuel Kleinhenn. He was employed by Kleinhenn for one year, and then in 1860, went into the employ of William Watt.

Here again is a point of some confusion. Julius Gemmer states that Watt was merely in charge of the Hawken business—city directories indicate he was actually owner by purchase. The choice of wording in his advertisements could hardly be interpreted otherwise.

At the outbreak of the War Between the States, Gemmer offered his services to the United States Government. He was given the rank of Corporal, and served as a gunsmith in the Government Arsenal, located in St. Louis. This arsenal, withs its 60,000 stand of arms, played a role of some importance in the early stages of the conflict.

While Julius Gemmer reports his father purchased the Hawken business from Samuel Hawken in 1862, the city directories continue to list Watt as proprietor and it is not until 1866 that Gemmer is listed as owner.

Here we may speculate a bit! We know nothing of Gemmer's financial background, but it is not likely that the son of a wealthy German emigrant would seek employment as an apprentice in a gun shop. Much more likely is the premise that the Gemmers were not wealthy, and that J. P. Gemmer had to seek such employment as he was best fitted for. Had he been supplied with sufficient capital, he could have become a merchant of guns, instead of maker and repairer of such merchandise. We feel fairly safe in our assumption that J. P. Gemmer was a poor boy, who had to start at the bottom, and by dint of hard work, and good management, made his way to the top. That he was able to acquire the Hawken business, and successfully continue it in a highly competitive business world is some indication of his ability.

The point we wish to make here is that in 1862, J. P. Gemmer, aged 24 years, had been in this country a mere seven years. Four years of that period had been spent as an apprentice, and another year in the employ of Kleinhenn. After another year of working for Watt, and then a year in the Government Arsenal, it would seem most unlikely that he was affluent enough to purchase a business such as the Hawken Manufactory. Much more likely is the premise that over a period of years, he was able to buy increasing shares of the business, until such time as he was able to assume full ownership.

Lacking full information concerning all the small details of the transaction, it is somewhat difficult to reconstruct the chain of events. Gemmer's commitment to the Government Arsenal undoubtedly prevented him from active participation in the Hawken business, so he would have had to rely heavily on a qualified person acting on his behalf. With the financial aspects of the business being bolstered by Gemmer's investments of cash, Watt would have been able to continue the business through the difficult war years. This writer's research has not brought to light just what part the Hawken shop played in contributing to the war effort. Quite likely they were plagued by the same shortages of material, lack of skilled help, and loss of markets that was the fate of other small businesses. Without the financial base of many successful years in business, William Watt could have come perilous close to losing his investment. In such an event, small but steady transfusion of capital by Gemmer might have been the thread that held the business intact. Since Gemmer did not marry until 1872, it would have been very possible for him to devote a major share of his income to such "transfusions," with full knowledge that eventually he would assume control of the business.

At the age of 34, Gemmer married Miss Louise Grewe, also of German parentage, and to them were

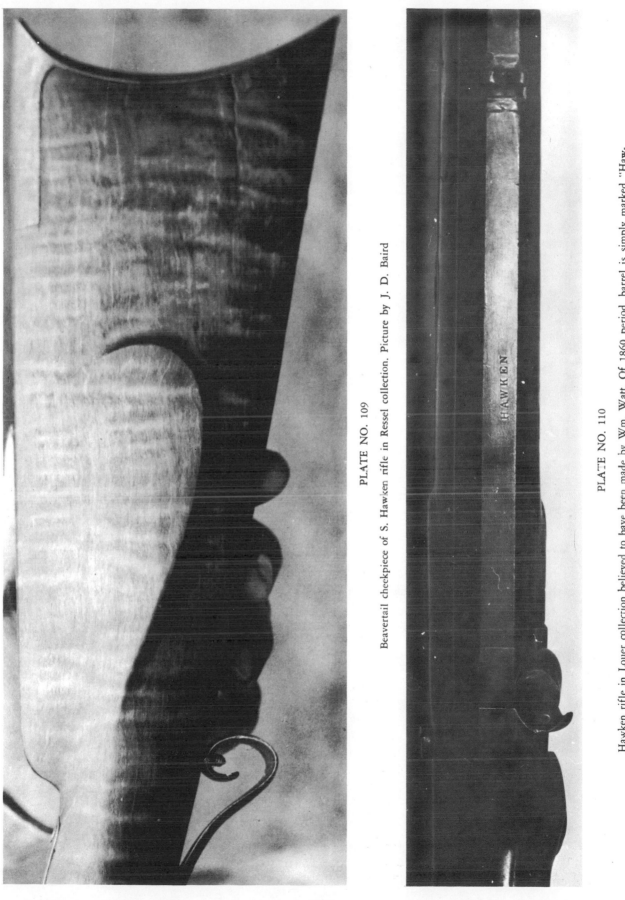

PLATE NO. 109

Beavertail cheekpiece of S. Hawken rifle in Ressel collection. Picture by J. D. Baird

PLATE NO. 110

Hawken rifle in Louer collection believed to have been made by Wm. Watt. Of 1860 period, barrel is simply marked "Hawken". Picture by E. M. Louer

73

born two children, First a daughter, named Adele, and then a son, whom they named Julius.

At the close of the Civil War, J. P. Gemmer was able to take his place as the proprietor of the Hawken Manufactory, and was to remain in that position until he closed the doors in retirement, some fifty years later. In October 1919, only four years after retiring, Mr. Gemmer passed away, and was buried in Bellefontaine Cemetery, not far from where Samuel Hawken had been buried some thirty years earlier.

Elsewhere in this volume, we have touched upon the impact breech-loading firearms were to have upon the gunmakers who had built their business around the production of muzzle-loading arms. This must have been a particularly difficult period for young Gemmer! Just getting established as owner of an old, highly esteemed muzzle-loading rifle manufactory, he was faced with the unrelenting competition of the breech-loader from the start. His skillful sporterizing of the Spencer carbine is an indication that he was aware of his need to keep pace in a rapidly changing world. While the demand for Hawken "Mountain Rifles" was to continue for quite some time, it was a steadily diminishing market, as new and better breech-loading arms came into use.

The brass case, with its centrally located primer, made possible the powerful, long ranged, single-shot breech-loaders that wrought such havoc among the buffalo herds. When the repeating rifles of Winchester and others could nearly equal the performance of the Sharps and Remington single-shots, the market for muzzle-loading rifles could only be among the Indian tribes. Even here it could not offer much, for the Indians were also quick to see the advantages of a rifle you could load today, and shoot all week. While it is established that the Indians armed themselves with whatever they could get their hands on, it is also true that they would expend any effort to acquire a Henry repeating rifle, and later exhibited the same enthusiasm for the Winchester when it was developed.

J. P. Gemmer faced up to this challenge with the enthusiasm of the young, and with the enterprise of his Germanic heritage. Elsewhere we have discussed the Spencer rilfes and how he "Hawkenized" them.

In the Missouri Historical Museum, of St. Louis, there is displayed a number of examples of his skill and enterprise. Over the years of being in the firearms business, Gemmer was able to build a fine collection of rare and beautiful guns. This collection was turned over to the Missouri Historical Society by his children upon his death, and are displayed to the public at the Jefferson Memorial Building in Forest Park.

Among those firearms displayed is one that has received the "Hawkenizing" treatment at the hands of Gemmer. Originally a trapdoor Springfield, it has been completely rebuilt, except for lock and breech. The original hammer has been replaced with the regular Hawken hammer, modified at the nose in order to strike a firing pin, rather than a percussion cap. Chambered for the 45-70 government cartridge, the breech remains unchanged in its function, but the barrel is octagon, and fitted with an underrib and guides for a cleaning rod. The stock is conventional Hawken halfstock pattern, with double set triggers and scroll guard of iron.

Among a number of guns in the display that are marked J. P. Gemmer, St. Louis, two are of particuar interest. At first glance they appear to be regular Hawken "Mountain Rifles," but a closer examination will reveal them to be very neatly made breech-loading cartridge guns. Differing in only minor details, both rifes are marked on the top barrel flat with the following inscription, "J. P. Gemmer St. Louis Pat applied for." Both rifles are chambered for the rimfire, bottle-necked .46 caliber Spencer cartridge.

The firing pin is housed in the patent breech section of barrel, emerging through an orifice where normally one would expect the nipple for a percussion cap to be, were the rifle a percussion fired 'Mountain Rifle." The breech is opened by raising a hinged block that is set into the barrel immediately ahead of the patent breech. This block is hinged to the barrel on its upper foremost edge, and swings up and forward much like the breech mechanism of the 1873 Springfield rifle. Other than the hinge feature, there is little resemblance to the breech of the Springfield, being much shorter, and having a much different arrangement for extracting the fired cases. An ingenious arrangement is used for locking the breech in place for firing.

The workmanship of these two rifles, as is the case

PLATE NO. 111

Grave of J. P. Gemmer, who continued Hawken tradition, and who went on to become famous as a gunsmith in his own right. Picture by T. K. Dawson

PLATE NO. 112

Stencil used by J. P. Gemmer from 1880 until 1915. From Ressel Collection. Photo by J. D. Baird.

with all such rifles marked J. P. Gemmer, is superb, showing great care and skill was employed in the making of these rifles. The placard with the exhibit states that Gemmer could not make these rifles by hand and successfully compete in a business that was being dominated by large companies mass producing guns through the use of machinery.

So, after more than sixty years of producing new guns, the old Hawken shop had to bow to the inevitable. No longer able to compete in the manufacture of breechloading guns, and the muzzle-loading "Mountain Rifles" relegated to status of relics," J. P. Gemmer was forced to reorganize his business so as to adapt it to the changing needs.

With skilled artisans in wood and metal in his employ, Gemmer was well situated to serve the growing number of gun "cranks" that were forever testing and seeking to improve the cartridge guns of the day. In his efforts to serve these customers, both as custom gunsmith, and supplier of ammunition and other sporting needs, he was able to expand these services into one of the major wholesale houses of sporting goods. Julius Gemmer states that his father's stock of loaded shells and metallic ammunition, which he bought by the carload, was depended upon for many years by the local jobbers for certain of their requirements. Horace Kephart, in his article in the April 1924 issue of the *American Rifleman,* speaks at great length about the Gemmer shop and of it being the favorite rendezvous of sportsmen and rifle "cranks".

Mr. Gemmer maintained the Hawken shop at the address of 21 Washington until construction of the Eads bridge across the Mississippi River forced him to find new quarters. In 1870, he located in 612 North Third Street, and then in 1874 moved to 600 North Third. In 1876 he moved the business again; this time to 764 North Third, and 1880 to 700 North Eighth Street. It was at this address that the business was closed by Mr. Gemmers retirement, thus bringing to a close one of the oldest firearms businesses in the United States at that time.

CHAPTER 13

Identifying And Dating Hawken Rifles

IN THE PRECEEDING chapters, we have attempted to bring out those bits of information concerning Hawken rifles that are not common knowledge. It is hoped that these efforts have enabled the readers to better understand the complexities of the Hawken epoch.

In the past few years, Hawken rifles have been discussed in a number of articles in various publications, but the very nature of a single article on any subject generally precludes the possibility of thoroughly covering the subject. The lead up, a general discussion of the main points, and then the closing of the article, along with space limitations, all tend to cause the author to condense what he has to say. Published work by most researchers has tended to conform to these limitations, resulting in the periodical reappearance of the Hawken story, in different words, and many times illustrated with full length pictures of such famous rifles as the one owned by Jim Bridger, or that of Kit Carson.

Both these rifles have been shown a number of times, and while such articles are well written, interesting, and very worthwhile, they tend to cause the reading public to obtain a fixed, and often incorrect concept of Hawken rifles. A general description is fine and necessary, but it does great injustice to the many Hawken rifles that do not conform to the description imposed by these very limited sources of information.

While very late Hawken rifles did tend to conform more to a set pattern, the great majority of the rifles produced in the Hawken shop varied widely in their construction details. That a recognizable style was followed is apparent, but details of construction varied so much that it is extremely difficult to give a description that can be applied to all Hawken rifles.

The main reason the late rifles come closer to being identical than earlier ones is because the adoption of cast parts in the 1850's left little room for the stockmaker's whim. It is in these rifles that we see so many different styles of cheekpieces; it being the only large area that could reflect the stockmaker's preference of style.

Wide, flat beaver tail forms, long narrow beavertail shapes, egg shaped cheekpieces, beavertails with paneled lower edges; all these forms reflect the skill and preference of the individual stockmaker. Many times the shape of the cheekpiece will help tell us who might have made the stock, and in so doing, help date that particular rifle.

As an illustration, a halfstock rifle stamped J. & S. Hawken, and presumably stocked by Jacob, will have a long narrow beavertail cheekpiece, occasionally with the bottom line forming a flute over the point where comb meets wrist. Very often, there will be an oval silver plate let into the face of the cheekpiece, held in place by either two silver nails, or two small iron screws.

On the other hand, rifles marked S. Hawken reflect a number of styles of cheekpieces, simply because a number of people made and sold the Hawken rifle. Samuel, his son William S. Hawken, William Watt, and J. P. Gemmer, all made rifles and stamped them S. Hawken, St. Louis. Tristam Campbell, while a partner to Sam in the years 1854-1858, undoubtedly contributed his share of variation in cheekpiece form. Certainly the highly engraved T. Campbell rifle in the William Almquist collection suggests Campbell's choice of cheekpiece shape to be that of oval form, with paneled bottom line.

Samuel Hawken seemed to prefer the wide, flat beavertail form, such as found on the Kephart Hawken, and on the last rifle he made. (This last rifle is on display at the Missouri Historical Museum at St. Louis.) This form, so much preferred by Sam, is the true beavertail cheekpiece. Watt, Gemmer, and Campbell made variations of this form, each according to his own taste.

While Sam may have used this form of cheekpiece on his fullstocked rifles, more often did he revert to the Tennessee style shown on the J. & S. Hawken pictured in Chapter 4. All the Hawken marked fullstocks that this writer has examined are fitted with this style of cheekpiece. Since Jake and Sam both learned their trade in their father's shop in Hagerstown, Maryland, the influence of their father, Christian Hawken, was no doubt being reflected when they were called upon to build a fullstocked rifle. Kaufman's book *"The Pennsylvania Kentucky Rifle"* has one plate showing the style of Christian Hawken, and this same basic style of

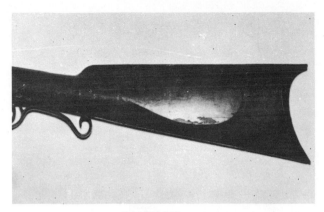

PLATE NO. 113

Cheekpiece of Horace Kephart's Hawken rifle, on display in Missouri Historical Museum, St. Louis. Courtesy Missouri Historical Society. Picture by T. K. Dawson

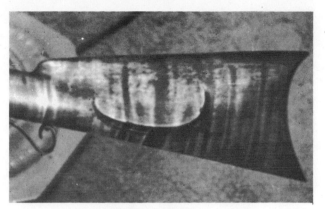

PLATE NO. 114

Panelled cheekpiece on S. Hawken rifle in the Leonard collection. Picture by J. D. Baird

cheekpiece is found on nearly all of his son's fullstocked rifles. It is only in their halfstocked rifles that their individual tastes were reflected in other cheekpiece forms.

It is this writer's personal opinion that the family relationship between Jake & Sam, played an important part in that partnership. He feels that in all probability, Sam was to play a minor role in the Hawken shop until after Jake's death. Being younger than Jake, little brother Sam could look after the business end of things, and it was big brother, Jake, who actually ran the shop, and determined the form the finished rifle would have. Certainly those rifles marked J. & S. Hawken, and therefore made before 1849, reflect a different influence than those made after that date.

After Jake's death, Samuel assumed full control and stamped the rifles S. Hawken, St. Louis. It is in these rifles that we see so many variants of form and construction detail. Modern, more efficient methods, castings, machine tools, standardization, all were grist in Sam's mill, as he fought to hold his market, and the reputation of Hawken for fine, dependable rifles.

Sam was faced with the problem of handling two men's work, plus the departure of Jake's son Christopher, and the unrelenting competition of Eastern makers like J. Henry and others. It is no small wonder that he was quick to adopt any method that would help produce Hawken rifles quicker and at less cost. With the gold rush in full swing, the market for guns was there, but the price of a Hawken was high, as compared to many Eastern maker's lists.

Cast buttplates, forend tips, breeches and rear sights, purchased barrel blanks, and even cast scroll trigger guards all were of great help in the more efficient production of rifles. Castings left less choice as to individual stock dimensions, and ultimately led to near standardization of the rifle's form, but it was a business man's way of keeping abreast of competition.

There were probably more Hawken rifles produced after Jacob Hawken's death than were made in all the plus thirty years that Jake was in control of things. While Sam kept the Hawken factory for only 10 years after Jake died, he had a much larger customer demand to serve, and Hawken rifles continued to be made until such rifles became unprofitable to manufacture. As late as 1894, Gemmer still had a few brand new Hawken rifles stored in a back room of his store. His refusal to sell them for less than the regular price, and the public's reluctance to pay so much for a mere relic in a modern cartridge gun era has made it possible for more than one gun collection to now have within it a S. Hawken rifle in near mint condition.

Let there be no mistake about J. P. Gemmer! Here was a gunsmith and rifle maker that needed to bow to no one. That he took such pains to continue making the traditional Hawken rifle is in itself a tribute to the rifle's reputation. His breech loading adaption to the Hawken style rifle is another indication of his respect for the Hawken rifle and the reputation it enjoyed.

Certainly he made other style rifles, shotguns, and even rifle-shotgun combination guns, but he stamped such pieces with his name. It was the halfstock of Sam and Jake that he continued stamping S. Hawken St. Louis. Cheekpieces, machine tool marks on hidden surfaces, castings, and his use of an adjustable rear sight are some of the clues when trying to determine who might have made any particular late style Hawken rifle.

The writer has been asked, "How are you able to arrive at a reasonable date of manufacture for whatever Hawken rifle you are examining?" To answer that question in print would be quite an undertaking, and then in all probability the answer would not be complete. It could not be completely conclusive, simply because no Hawkens were dated as to year of manufacture. However, there are a great many clues that enable

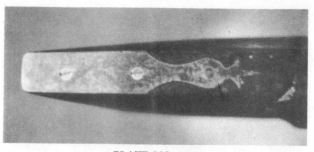

PLATE NO. 115

Fancy toeplate on S. Hawken rifle in Wm. Almquist collection. Picture by J. D. Baird

us to make an intelligent guess. While we have touched on this subject before, it may not be amiss to mention a few things that help determine when a specific rifle was made.

Since Jacob worked alone from 1815 to 1822, it must be assumed that there were no J. & S. Hawken marked rifles marketed prior to 1822. After his death May 8, 1849, Samuel marked all rifles S. Hawken, St. Louis. Therefore, we have the dates 1822 to 1849 to work with when examining a rifle marked J. & S. Hawken. In this period of 27 years, the percussion system was undergoing a rapid development. Those developments could not help but be reflected in progressive improvements in the breech section of the Hawken. Rifles that have various attempts at ornamentation give other clues as to when they might have been made.

Tristam Campbell, a fine engraver, is first listed as being in the employ of the J. & S. Hawken shop in 1842. After this date, J. & S. Hawken rifles with engraved patchboxes, tangs, and trigger guards were available. It is remarkable that the Modena rifle, known to have been purchased before this date, with considerable ornamentation, nevertheless has no engraving. The reason was that no one in the shop before 1842 was capable of doing that type of work. With just a little arithmetic, we find that engraved J. & S. Hawken rifles were available for only about seven years. Keeping in mind that from 1845 to 1849 Tristam Campbell and C. Hoffman were listed at a separate address from that of the Hawken shop, we may presumably again narrow the time span involved.

The writer wishes to point out that no one feature of a rifle is in itself conclusive in making an estimate of the date of manufacture. There are a great many variables that can alter the case, and it is only after a thorough study of many rifles that the characteristics of early or late manufacture are apparent.

While we repeat, no single feature is in itself conclusive, it is interesting to note that the simple expedient of holding the lower thimble to stock underwent no less than three seperate methods of attachment.

Close examination of early rifles will reveal that the lower thimble was held in place with two round pins passing through the stock. Midway in the Hawken period, the use of two pins was dropped, and the thimble held in place by a single pin. Ultimately the use of the pin was dropped, and the thimble held in place by a screw passing through the stock from under the barrel. The cast iron forend tip of these late rifles was retained by the same manner.

Another area of interest is the buttplate. The J. & S. Hawken rifle usually had a rather flat crescent, with the lower edge of the top piece forming a distinct curve where it joined the crescent. When the cast buttplate was adopted, this curving line was dropped in favor of a straight bottom edge. Rifles of distinctive late features, but equipped with the early style buttplate, posed for a time somewhat of a puzzle to this writer. However, the opportunity to remove the buttplates of some of these rifles revealed that they too were castings. Mold marks indicated that the early style, handmade buttplate had been used for a pattern. Therefore, we now examine the buttplate very closely to ascertain if it be handmade, or a casting. The handmade buttplate will almost invariably show a faint line of brass where the crescent is joined to the top piece.

Tristam Campbell, who went into business for himself at 76 Locust Street, upon Sam's disposing of the Hawken shop, made mountain type rifles stamped T. Campbell, St. Louis. The engraved, silver inlayed specimen in the William Almquist collection needs be mentioned here because it is fitted with such a buttplate as described above. Whether such metal casting was being done in St. Louis or back East is a matter of conjecture. Seemingly, Campbell, being familiar with this style of plate, and having access of it, preferred to use it on his rifles.

Incidently, Campbell, in spite of many years association with the Hawken shop, had a style of his own when he made rifles in his own shop. In a comparison between his rifles and those made in the Hawken shop,

PLATE NO. 116

Small steamboat, "Golden Arrow", tied to Chouteau's Landing, at St. Louis. Picture by T. K. Dawson

PLATE NO. 117

Photographic reproduction of Barsotti's "Mountain Men and Hawken Rifles." Courtesy John Barsotti. Picture by J. D. Baird

one thing is certain. There would be no mistaking a Campbell rifle for being a Hawken. While they show a great deal of Hawken influence, Campbell's use of silver, his engraving, and his style of stock shaping cause his rifles to reflect his own personal taste.

We have often mentioned "unmarked" Hawken rifles. Such terminology is a source of irritation to many gun collectors, and not a few hold the opinion that "they ain't no such animal!" While recognizing and appreciating their position, the writer will reiterate his convictions on this controversial subject.

Hawken rifles were hand made, under rather primitive conditions, as compared to rifle factories of later days. While a great many were made to the specifications set forth by the buyer, many more were made for the market, so to speak, to be sold off the shelf. Made for a period of over fifty years, by assorted artisans, the rifles, while retaining a recognizable style, do show individual characteristics. A thorough study of these characteristics will result in the student being able to recognize and evaluate those individual rifles, almost independently of the barrel markings.

We are well aware that here we are treading dangerous ground. We would be the first to exclaim that certainly not all unmarked halfstock rifles are Hawken rifles. Nor are they necessarily even "Plains" rifles. Neither do we wish to appoint ourselves judge and jury over what is, and what it not "Hawken." We merely wish to point out that such unmarked rifles were sold, and we feel that more of them are still in existence than is generally realized. How to recognize them, authenticate them, and assimilate them into their rightful place in Hawken collections are problems to be solved.

If a rifle was made in the Hawken shop, in the Hawken style, it is a Hawken, whether made by Jake, Sam, Watt, or Gemmer. St. Louis makers like Dimmick, Klienhenn, and others did not make "Hawken" rifles, even though they may have adopted Hawken features. Watt and Gemmer, however, were deliberate in their efforts to continue making rifles in the Hawken tradition, and their product can only be called Hawken guns.

When J. P. Gemmer built rifles of his own design, differing from the Hawken style, he stamped them with his name. The rifles he made in the Hawken tradition, or style, call it what you will, he marked with the name S. Hawken. Our personal opinion is that a Spen-

PLATE NO. 118

Harold "Bill" Fuller, gunsmith of Coopers Landing, Alaska, shown holding a .54 caliber S. Hawken rifle equipped with Leman lock. Rifle is owned by Dick Johnston. Photograph furnished by H. Fuller

cer rifle sporterized by Gemmer in the Hawken tradition, is no less a Hawken rifle than is a percussion "Mountain Rifle" made by him (Gemmer), and stamped S. Hawken.

To make a point—a Winchester rifle is just that, whether made under Oliver Winchester, or long after his death. A Hi-Standard rifle is also just that, and the name Sears Roebuck on the barrel does not alter who made it.

We will qualify our statements in one regard. We seriously doubt if many unmarked rifles were sold prior to 1850. After that date, particularly when the economy was in one of its periodic slumps, rifles were sold where and however they could be marketed. The varying degrees of quality lead us to think that a great many small bore rifles, cheaply made, and low in price, constituted a source of bread and butter for the Hawken shop. The increasing competition from the new breech-loading rifles would increase the need to find, and supply, new markets, wherever they might be.

CHAPTER 14

Modern Hawken Replicas

WITH THE GREATLY increased interest in "Plains" rifles, or more properly, "Mountain Rifles," and particularly the Hawken, there is also manifested a desire to own and shoot such a rifle. For most of us, this means a Hawken replica, and more than likely, one that is largely home-built. We include this chapter for the benefit of those who are suffering from the urge to build such a rifle, and desire a bit of information on how best to proceed.

When an accurate copy of a Hawken rifle is attempted, trouble rears its ugly head almost immediately. While there are many small details of design and workmanship that are immensely important to the dedicated builder, one of the more disastrous errors is of a more general nature. This misinterpretation of the rifle's general description; resulting in having prominent characteristics greatly over-emphasized. It is well to bear in mind that any description of a Hawken rifle can be more deceptive than revealing.

It has often been said that a Hawken was a big, heavy rifle. True! It is also said that it had a short, thick barrel, stocked with a generous amount of wood. Sometimes true again, but one must consider in what frame of reference the writer is speaking. As a rule, descriptions of a Hawken are given against the background of the Kentucky squirrel rifle; it being the accepted standard rifle of the period. Using the Kentucky rifle as a yardstick, one can say that the Hawken was 10-15% larger. As for weight, the Hawken might weigh half again more than the Kentucky. The barrel could be anywhere from twenty-eight to forty-eight inches in length, but the average would be thirty-five inches against forty inches for the Kentucky. The buttstock of a Hawken is larger; in that it has greater vertical depth, but the thickness of the buttplate will average about one and one quarter inches, not much wider than the Kentucky.

A casual inspection of the forearm of a Hawken rifle might give the impression that there is considerable wood in this area. There is, of course, but when you figure that inside that forearm there is a barrel of about 1 1/8 inches across the flats, and a 1/2 inch ram-rod that has to clear a pair of keys and heavy barrel lugs, you realize that there is no more wood than is absolutely necessary. In fact the tolerance and clearance figures are comparable to the slimest of Kentucky rifles. If one should proceed on the assumption that a Hawken stock has plenty of wood and hence does not require close grouping of components, he will invariably end up with an oversize stock that is not at all typical of Hawken work.

The first requisite for building a Hawken rifle is to determine the style and period of rifle one prefers, get all the information possible on this type, and then follow this style religiously. Hawken rifles changed somewhat through the plus-40 years of their manufacture, and to be authentic, one should not have an 1860 style forend tip or Gibbons style lock on an 1835 J. & S. Hawken replica. Occasionally we find a Hawken rifle that has been re-worked at the Hawken factory, with such mixing of parts as late barrels equipped with early sights, late breech let into a tang of earlier style, etc. To those who have handled a great number of Hawken rifles, such variations are quickly noted, and easily understood.

We speak here of more subtle variations. For instance—the Modena rifle, or for that matter, any J. & S. Hawken marked rifle. Use any good picture of such a rifle, and lay a straight edge along the top line of the comb. You will see a slight arch in this line—just a suggestion of a Roman nose shape. Not really a Roman nose, yet enough to suggest that Jake's early training in his father's shop is showing through.

The later rifles, marked S. Hawken, will not have this slight arch. The top line of the comb on these rifles will form a straight line.

Compare pictures of rifles marked J. & S. Hawken, and those marked S. Hawken. See the difference in the shaping around the lock panels! Note also that J. & S. Hawken marked rifles will generally use rectangular heads on the barrel keys, whereas S. Hawken rifles will use oval heads. Another point; the lower thimble on J. & S. Hawken rifles will be held in place with two pins, later rifles used one, and then even later ones went to a screw through the forearm from beneath the barrel. Note such differences as shape of cheekpiece

on the differently marked rifles, the transition of rear sights, use of patchboxes, and other attempts at ornamentation.

A good, reliable stock pattern can be obtained from a 35 mm negative, but a regular transparency serves much better. Cast your projection upon a large sheet of white paper, adjusting the projector until your picture is the exact size of the original rifle. Check for distortion by comparing measurements in a number of areas. When you are satisfied that your projection is perfect, carefully copy the projected image. If you have rubbings, it is well to use them to help you determine if your projected image is correct.

A shortcut to the above procedure is to obtain one of the full-size Hawken drawings that is available from such supply houses as Wes Kindig's Log Cabin Sport Shop, in Lodi, Ohio. Wes also has a full-size photograph, with several views, of a S. Hawken rifle. These aids will prove to be most helpful, well worth the modest cost.

The prospective rifle builder has studied his subject, determined the style Hawken rifle he desires, and has made up his stock pattern. His selection of hardware should reflect his choice of the style and period rifle he is about to duplicate.

We will assume that you have the barrel and other hardware on hand, and are ready to make the stock. If your barrel is average; say 1 1/8 inch across the flats at the breech, the stock thickness will be close to 1 3/4 inch. Use a jointer and planer to bring the blank to correct thickness and square the top surface to the sides.

Lay the stock pattern on the plank with top of the barrel line against the squared top surface. Mark the stock outline. (The Hawken shop cut their blanks so that the grain of the wood ran lengthwise through the wrist.) The next step is to figure the required depth of the forend. This will be width of the barrel, plus depth of rib (which determines ram-rod to barrel spacing) plus diameter of rod, plus about 1/8th of an inch for wood to cover the ram-rod on the bottom. After you have this measurement figured, mark this line on the blank. Now make another line about 1/4 inch below and parrallel to this line. This extra wood gives some leeway if things go astray, and gives support while drilling the ram-rod hole. Cut the outline of the stock, using this second line, (not the finish line) for the forestock.

Inlet the barrel and tang. Install lugs and keys. It is much easier to drill the blank for the keys while the sides are still straight, a drill-press comes in handy here. If you do not have one, no matter. Just proceed with much caution. With the barrel properly inletted, attach ram-rod guide rib.

The easiest form of forend tip to make is the cast-in-place type. A lead-tin mixture serves very well for this, and should be cast as a large block. With the rib for a guide, now drill the ram-rod hole through this block, and length ways through the stock-blank.

Cut away lower half of cast forend tip, shape tip and wood of forend, and install lower thimble. Next, using rasp and planes, cut away the extra 1/4 inch of wood on the bottom of the forend. If all has went well,

PLATE NO. 121

Author's attempt at copying trigger guard found on rifle described in Chapter 3. Guard was made by welding easily bent scroll to old shotgun guard. Picture by J. D. Baird

PLATE NO. 122

Modern copy of Hawken triggers and guard assembly Picture by J. D. Baird

and the drill ran straight, you should be able to remove 1/4 inch of wood, and still have 1/8 inch of wood over the ram-rod channel. Sit down and smoke a cigarette. If everything is fine, you've earned it. If not, don't despair. You can install a wear plate on the bottom of the forend to hide the boo-boo. If the hole came out the side, smoking privileges have been suspended.

We are now ready to mark the location of the lock panels. The panels taper, being wider in front than at the rear; in this case 1 3/4 inches at the front, and 1 5/8 inches at the rear. Give the blank the correct taper in this area. Now fit the buttplate to the right side of the stocks—usually 1/4 inch to the right of center line. This provides wood for the cheekpiece and gives the correct amount of cast-off. Mark guide lines from buttplate to barrel and rough shape the buttstock and cheekpiece. Install the lock and trigger assembly. Shape up the lock panels, and wrist area. You now have a basic Hawken rifle that requires only finishing to your taste.

There are a few characteristics of a Hawken that are not readily apparent from a study of photographs. The buttstock is quite deep vertically, but comparatively thin, however, in no case was it like a board, and did not appear slab-sided. The point of the comb at the wrist is very thin, nearly knife edged, quite similiar to the Sharp's rifle.

Hawken rifles rarely have any pronounced sharp edges on the wood, as in the carving that forms the outline of the lock panels. The edge is rounded and somewhat blurred. The wrist is not round, but elliptical with greater diameter vertically than horizontally. There is very seldom much wood covering the side of the barrel, usually 1/8 inch or less, and this tapers in somewhat in from the foreward key through the forend tip.

A Hawken was developed from butt to muzzle to be purely functional. It was strong but not bulky, moderately heavy but well balanced and exceedingly compact. It is essential to bear in mind that it was not extreme in any of its characteristics, and that it is very easy to "overdo it" when making a reproduction.

Those few words we have used above describe the basic steps in reproducing the halfstock Hawken rifle. Should the prospective builder desire a fullstocked rifle, the essential steps are the same. A sheet iron forend tip is used on the fullstock models, and the use of escutcheons for the barrel keys are dispensed with.

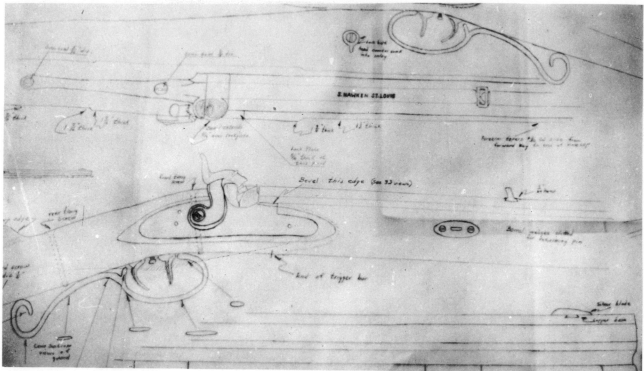

PLATE NO. 123

Pencil drawings of details of late S. Hawken rifle, for purposes of reproducing such rifles with accuracy. Picture by J. D. Baird

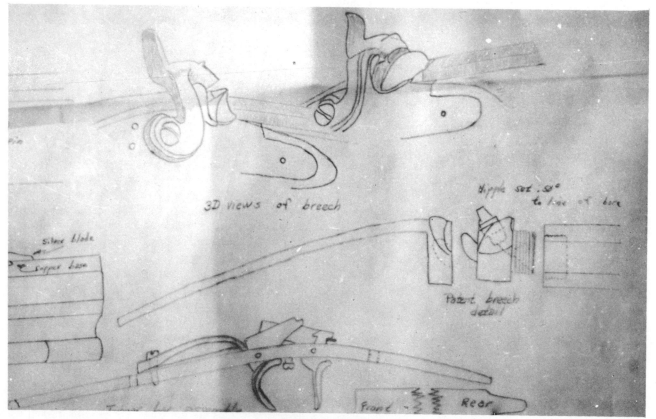

PLATE NO. 124

Another view of drawings of S. Hawken rifle. Picture by J. D. Baird

PLATE NO. 125

Pencil drawings of J&S Hawken fullstock described in Chapter 4. Picture by J. D. Baird

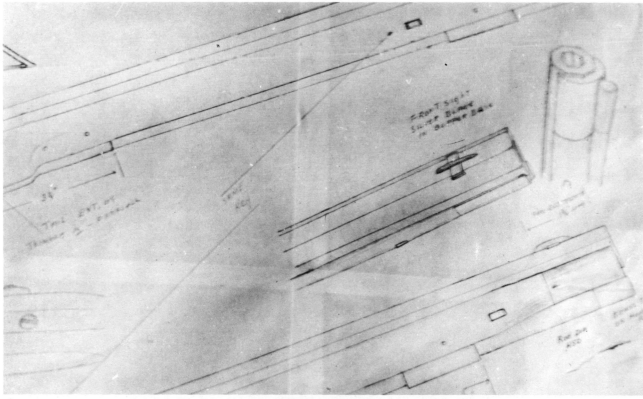

PLATE NO. 126

Pencil drawings of barrel details on J&S Hawken fullstock rifle from Orville Dunham collection. Picture by J. D. Baird

PLATE NO. 127

T. K. Dawson, holding one of his early attempts at duplicating a Hawken Mountain Rifle. Mr. Dawson and the author of this book have spent many pleasurable hours discussing Hawken rifles, examining them, building them, and shooting them.

While the writer has examined a number of brass mounted Hawken rifles, in every case they were special purpose guns. The regular "Mountain Rifle" was invariably mounted with iron fixtures. Some of the early Hawken Mountain Rifles were mounted in brass, but having no information other than our personal experience, we cannot offer anything on this. Those brass mounted rifles we have examined were either light squirrel rifles for the local St. Louis trade, or heavy target rifles, not suited for the use they would receive in the hands of a trapper or Mountain Man.

Those muzzle-loading rifle enthusiasts who belong to the National Muzzle Loading Rifle Association, receive each month, a copy of *Muzzle Blasts,* the official magazine of that organization. This little magazine has steadily improved over the years, and is jam-packed with information of all kinds, pertaining to muzzle-loading guns. Its advertisements give the reader a wide choice

of sources for components, should he wish to build such a rifle, and among the pages of *Muzzle Blasts* will be found the information on how to load and shoot the finished gun, where he can find like-interested friends to shoot with, and the results of those matches, whether they be formal or impromptu. The articles on shooting, building rifles and researched material on old guns and their makers are a continuing source of interest. We heartily recommend that those who are interested in old guns, or the history of our American heritage, send six dollars and a letter of application for membership to the NMLRA, Box 15, Friendship, Indiana 47021.

Somewhere in our literary peregrinations, we recall having seen the statement that early rifle makers in Pennsylvania had a recipe for rifle components. Briefly it ran, "Barrel by Remington, Lock from Golcher, and Fixings from Tyron." We mention it in passing only because our own efforts at reproducing a "Mountain

"Carson's Men," an oil painting by Charles Russell at Thomas Gilcrease Institute, Tulsa, Oklahoma.

Rifle" have subscribed to a similar recipe. This one reads, Barrel by Large, Lock by Roller and Fixings from Kindig.

Every rifle that we have made, admittedly not great in number, was built around a barrel either recut by Bill Large, or new made to our specifications by that worthy producer of rifled tubes. Bill's JJJJ Ranch, Gun & Machine Shop in Ironton, Ohio, has long been known as the source for the finest handmade rifle barrels.

We count Bob Roller, of Huntington, W. Virginia, among our friends, and we know Roller locks grace modern made muzzle-loaders from Virginia to Alaska.

His latest addition to his line of locks, a perfect copy of a T. Gibbons lock as found on late Hawken rifles, will find a welcome reception among rifle builders.

The first streak of rust that we sent to Bill Large for salvage work came from the shop of Wes Kindig, many years ago, and since then, triggers, buttplates, and fixings of all kinds have continued to come from that source. The Log Cabin Sport Shop, Lodi, Ohio, has long catered to the modern muzzle-loading rifle builder, and was the very first to recognize the interest in Hawken, and attempt to supply components for such rifles.

CHAPTER 15

Miscellany

THIS, THE FINAL chapter, could very well be considered an afterthought, and if it appears to be a hodge-podge of ideas, thoughts, and expressions, perhaps it appears so because it is just that. In the space of time between typing the last line of chapter fourteen, and getting the manuscript to the printer, those little bits of information, photographs, and correspondence that came to hand were of sufficient value to cause us to wish them included in the book. A miscellany of bits and pieces, they present somewhat of a problem, as to how best to work them into a manuscript that, to all intents, had been put into final form weeks before. It was decided to add on a chapter, much as a home sometimes has a small room built on to serve as storeroom for those bits and pieces of furnishing that, while not offering any immediate value to the household, still represent too much value to be discarded. So it is with the contents of this chapter. We found these tidbits to be of interests; perhaps the reader will be of like mind, and even find a bit of humor in an otherwise dull book.

As was mentioned in the introduction, our early attempts at learning of Hawken rifles met with much frustration. Then, greatly to our pride, we reached that point where we were sure that we knew all there was to know about the subject. How very surprised we were, when we learned that we actually knew very little, and since then, have become more and more aware that the more we learn, the less we know, in relation to the whole subject. The blooming thing seemingly grows, and as new information comes to our attention, so also do new avenues, new sources, new ideas, all to be explored, assimilated, and our thinking changed to adjust to this new information. If nothing else, we have learned to keep an open mind, always on the lookout for a wrinkle that had not occured to us before. Some of the best friends we have were acquired through correspondence, while exploring those avenues opened by research, and we offer some of that correspondence, partly to show how one can learn through exchange of ideas, and partly to share the humor sometimes found in our mailbox.

As was mentioned in Chapter 14, Bill Large has long

been one of these craftsmen whom we have admired, and considered a friend. After sending a number of old, pitted, disreputable streaks of rust to Bill for re-cutting, Bill lost patience with me and wrote that I should quit messing around with that old junk, and build my rifles using his new "Plainsman" barrel. His

PLATE NO. 129

William "Bill" Large, Ironton, Ohio, gunsmith, barrel-maker, shooter, and one of the small group who founded the National Muzzle-loading Rifle Association. Picture furnished courtesy of Wm. Large

propensity for scribbling a note without dating it makes it somewhat difficult to arrange his correspondence in proper chronological order, but sometime in the spring of 1959, we received a long package in the mail, with a letter attached that read—

"If you can't see your way clear to pay for this, then return at once, collect.

Bill

This is my $50.00 barrel, so send me $40.00 as a special favor to a Plainsman nut."

By judicious juggling of pocket money, curtailed use of cigarettes, and other such drastic measures, ultimately the money was found for the barrel, and it, a very fine piece of work in .58 caliber, was soon stocked up in the best Hawken style we were capable of. While our stocking efforts left much to be desired, the barrel served admirably, and a 125 grain charge of 2ff caused it to speak authoritatively among the local groundhog population. A .575 ball leaves a groundhog somewhat shaken; usually the victim's tail extends straight into the air, and twirls at an amazing speed, after being struck by such a missile.

A two week camping trip in the hills of Brown County, of Southern Indiana, gave us further opportunity to learn of this caliber's potential. While we never got a chance to see if we really would shoot a deer out of season, no Indian ever stalked a trail with more care, or approached a rub with more caution. But two weeks of running the ridges and following trails in heavy timber, all on foot, with full mountain man equipment, gave us new insight into the activities of those hardy souls. A twelve pound rifle, a heavy knife, and a hunting bag filled with .58 caliber balls, a horn full of powder, and those accessories necessary to care for the rifle—all combined to drive home the convictions that the pouch strap should be wider, and a horse would be a very desirable animal to own, meriting the very best of care. It was also noted, after sliding down some inclines on our bottom, that the soles of our moccasins tended to wear slick on leaf covered trails. Moss, grass and leaves, all came to be regarded with a wary eye, and the bare trail, or sandy stream bed were welcomed with the same manner our fathers must have welcomed the paved highways, after driving for miles in muddy ruts.

Lee Good, of Tulsa, Oklahoma, whose wife, Mary Elizabeth, is on the Public Relations Committee of the National Muzzle-loading Rifle Association, confided to me, during a visit to Tulsa, that all correspondence his wife receives from Bill Large is addressed—

Mary Elizabeth Good

The Next Congresswoman from Oklahoma

While we have no way of knowing how many postmasters about the country are puzzled by envelopes bearing such addresses, we do know that the post mistress in Pence has long become enured to seeing letters arrive bearing the message—

To: John Dinglehofer Baird
King of the Wild Frontier
Iffen in deep study, don't
disturb, might break sompin

or a variation of the above theme. On what basis we were accorded the name of Dinglehofer, we have never been able to ascertain, but rather than be insulted, we have chosen to feel honored that a busy man would assign us special notice. We have treasured those envelopes, and their contents, and often turn to them for the chuckle they invariably provide. As a signal of our approbation, we requested that Bill stamp our .53 caliber barrel, acquired this winter, with such an inscription.

Eccentric! Perhaps, but the Brown County farmer who caught Tom Dawson and the writer in his pasture that summer, while dressed in our best mountain man style, thought we were a bit more than eccentric! Only his awe of two long, muzzle-loading rifles, and our respect for his double barrel shotgun, kept the meeting on a friendly basis, and we parted company with the two of us hurrying to the fence we should not have crossed, and the farmer returning to his house, shaking his head at what you could find in the woods these days.

Over the years that we have been interested in muzzle-loading guns, and particularly those made by Jake and Sam Hawken, we have found many occasions to seek the opinion of Bill Large. With the vast number of old barrels that he has recut, it was only natural that he should have occasion to work on a Hawken barrel.

PLATE NO. 130

Robert May, Chapman, Nebraska, holding his original J&S Hawken .55 caliber halfstock rifle. Note that about 6 inches has been cut from muzzle end of gun. Picture furnished courtesy of R. May

He informed us that his first recutting of a Hawken barrel took place in 1929 or 30, and that he has recut from 25 to 30 since then. Bill's lifelong experiences with many thousands of old barrels should put him in a unique position of being able to correctly appraise any barrel marked Hawken, St. Louis. We offer the following quotation from one of his letters as being the opinion of a well qualified expert.

"I find Hawken barrels mostly made out of what old timers called plain, dead iron, bend slightly and it is bent, no spring. Some were copper-steel, and it was dead iron too. Some of black iron, this is harder. I find none like the Great Western Gun Works generally made, copper-steel and full of flaws and crawfish holes. The average twist is 7 grooves, one turn in 48", some of the latest 6 grooves, a turn in 48" and I don't think they were of before 1850 vintage. Grooves run 12 to 14 thousandths deep and mostly about equal, and in some cases lands wider than the furrows. All were belled and showed signs of the funneling tool commonly used by most gun smiths, as a request of the owner, to permit easy and fast reloading. They were all choked, mostly a gradual choke, this is done with the common cutting operation, in the hands of a skilled craftsman, knowing how to use one; sort of sixth sense, by feeling and doing what you want as you work.

On one of our visits with Bill, we mentioned those barrels plainly marked on the top flat as being a Hawken, yet having other names stamped on the underside. One case coming to mind is the J. & S. Hawken in the Leonard collection, that carries the name H. W. Reeds, Reading Pa. stamped on the underflat of the barrel. Bill concurred in our opinion that with the advent of English cast steel for gun barrels, the Hawken shop would recognize the superior qualities of barrels made by this process, and as a result, purchased a great number of such blanks from eastern sources, doing the rifling in their own shop.

While sharing our interest in Hawken rifles with the readers of *Muzzle Blasts* magazine, reader correspondence opened up a number of avenues of exploration, and several Hawken rifles "discovered" that had heretofore remained unknown to the general public. It soon became apparent that the prices for Hawken rifles were going up, and we were often asked to place a value on a particular piece. Throughout our studies, we have been careful to refrain from this very thing; feeling that it was not in our province to tell anyone what his rifle was worth, or not worth, as the case might be. Ours was strictly a research project, to find more information on those rifles, and it could only end in disaster if we

allowed ourselves to be diverted down such a path. We took such a position shortly after an episode in which we suggested that a fine J. & S. Hawken rifle could not be worth less than $1500, only to learn that the owner had been about to sell it to an eager buyer for $500.00. Now we contain our remarks about values to what we know various rifles to have sold for, and leave the pricing to those active in the trade. We take comfort in the thought that we, somewhat in the manner of Thoreau, own every Hawken rifle we have examined, yet have no need to dust, clean, or fear for the safety of any of them. We can view them at any moment, compare them, shoot them, and share the campfire with their whiskery, leather-clad owners, yet move not a whit from our comfortable chair. Could a wall full of guns, or a bank vault filled with Hawken rifles give us more pleasure?

John Barsotti's painting *"Mountain Men and Hawken Rifles"* hangs on the wall over our desk, and a sketch of the riverboat "The Golden Eagle" over that. To our left hangs a display of flint arrowheads, and a hunting pouch and horn, in company with our "Hawken" rifle. Stuck to the wall is a postcard picture of the frontier store at Cooper's Landing, Alaska. We need only lift our eyes, and we are transported to such places as St. Louis, the Great Plains, the Missouri River, or even to the wilderness of Alaska's Kenai Peninsula. Could it be the first hints of approaching old age that suggest this to be the most comfortable way to travel. And what jet plane, however fast, could whisk you back to a mountain stream, complete with beaver dam, buffalo ribs roasting before the fire, and Blackfoot tepees in the background? The writer rode a Mustang down the Santa Fe Trail, from Bent's Fort to Taos, and to Santa Fe. What matter if the Mustang was born and reared in the Ford plant at Detroit, and not roped and broke by a Ogallala brave.

The trading posts that served Carson and his contemporaries may now carry goods marked Made in Japan, but we did not notice, or if we did, could conveniently disregard it. The sun was in the same place, and the mountains had not changed, and a man still had no business being afoot between La Junta and Trinidad. Our Mustang had plenty of water, but we darn well thought he was going to run out of gas before we got to the next station. The fact that our Hawken lay behind the seat, instead of across the saddle made very little difference, when we came down from the Raton Pass. A traffic check would have recorded us as being there in 1967, but to us, the year was 1847, and that big diesel rig, pulling two trailers, that we passed, was really a 20-mule team of the Santa Fe traders, with two huge Conestoga wagons, filled with goods for the Spanish trade.

That we are not alone in such daydreaming is ap-

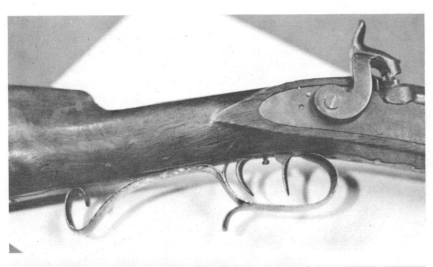

PLATE NO. 131

Late Hawken rifle in the Arthur Ressel collection, having a spur on the scroll trigger guard, much like the guards found on the J&S Hawken pistols in the Wm. Locke collection. Picture by J. D. Baird

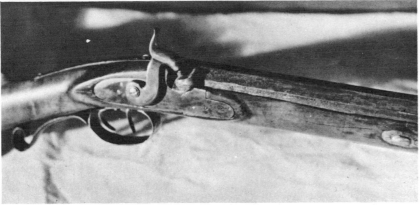

PLATE NO. 132

.45 caliber Hawken rifle in the Veit collection. This is one of those rifles having the Hawken name obliterated by overstamping repeatedly with the St. Louis stamp. Picture by J. D. Baird

PLATE NO. 133

Spencer-Hawken o w n e d by Merrill Deer, being unusual in that the original buttstock was retained, and the conversion consisting of new barrel, stamped S. Hawken, St. Louis, new sights, new forend, tip, two keys, and other features of the Hawken rifle. Rifle is .52 caliber, and breech is not marked with issue date, as are most of these conversions. Picture by J. D. Baird

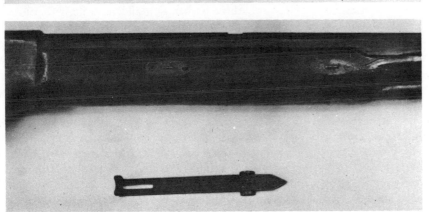

PLATE NO. 134

Spencer-Hawken in Deer collection, showing forearm detail, and long leaf rear sight. Sight appears to be original, but hides barrel stamp when placed in barrel. Picture by J. D. Baird

PLATE NO. 135

David Baird, author's son, holds his father's replica of a Hawken mountain rifle. Photo by J. D. Baird.

parent when we read letters from some of our fellow Hawken enthusiasts. In one of many letters between the writer and Bob May, of Chapman, Nebraska, we remarked that we were a bit sick of the weather. In fact, we stated, "Durn the country, and the weather, wisht I was at the Planters House, in ole St. Louey, a gaming, and a groggin, with a wench or two to liven up the party, a good dog in the pot. Greenup will come, reckin, but seems fur off!"

Friend Bob falls into the mood at once, and fires a letter right back, saying, "That Planters House idea of yours shines! Me, I'll take Taos! Plenty of game, all the old campanieros, and none of them city booshway; and where can you get better Taos lightnin, then right thar in Taos.

"Sounds as iffen you be having winter fur sartin sure. It be a mite cold here too. Looked out this mornin, and seed two bunnies pushing a jack, trying to get him started."

Those who find old guns interesting, must have a particular screw loose, somewhere, to find their pleasures in such odd manner. Who but an antique gun nut would understand when we speak of the thrill we felt, just at sunrise one summer day, when we visited New Salem, Illinois. With a thin streamer of ground fog wafting among the trees, the only sounds those of the hungry oxen penned behind the wool mill, and some sheep in a small pasture; the whole scene was one that could make the beholder feel that at any moment, the occupants of those cabins would be up and about. Later in the morning, as the grounds became thronged with tourists, the spell was broken, but for a few moments, we saw an early American village, as it really must have been.

Some of our postal friends have no need to resort to dreaming to see themselves in a log cabin, a river

before their door, and a mountain peering over their shoulder. Bill Fuller, of Cooper's Landing, Alaska, lives in such a setting. His letters speak calmly of 30 and 40 degrees below, and of moose feeding beside his 200 yard target, or sleeping in his back yard. Bill is a Hawken fan, and builds a few rifles, as time permits. Equipped with a few modern machine tools, he has come to understand and respect the craftsmanship put into building such a rifle. To duplicate such work, even with modern tools, taxes the skill of the best, and elicits the highest admiration for those workmen in the Hawken shop.

We will not attempt to describe Bill as being meticulous— he is, as is readily apparent to those who know of his jubilation at learning how the Hawken shop produced buttplates for their rifles. Quite by accident, it was discovered that they made the crescent and the heel as two pieces, then joined them with a rivet. In the cavity formed by the two pieces, brass and flux was placed, then the assembly placed in the forge and heat applied until the brass flowed. Upon flowing of the brass, the joint was made, and a file or grinder quickly removed the excess.

Living in the land of moose and Kodiak bear, it is understandable that Bill Fuller's rifles tend to be .58 caliber, and he speaks knowingly of 180 grain charges for these rifles. Our comment—"Wagh!" We have promised to witness such a shot being fired, but submit that we may not have the nerve to take our turn at the shooting bench.

A game warden in Oregon, a trout hatcheryman in Ruby Valley, Nevada; a medical supply salesman in St. Louis, a doctor in Alton, or Garrison, a plumber from Grand Island, a dentist from Cedar Rapids, and civil engineers from Lathrop Village, San Jose, or Pasadena—all express the same enthusiasm, and exhibit the symptoms of being bitten by the same bug. Good useful citizens, every one, but each will confess that his wife thinks he spends an awful lot of time in the workshop.

Bless those patient souls, for they know, even though they understand not, that but for a mere hundred years, those faithful husbands would have been found in the Bayou Salade, or Taos, or wintering in Bent's Fort. They know that time is on their side, and they can be generous. If their man goes to work in the morning, and comes home in the evening, what matter the few hours each evening he becomes a mountain man, in spirit, if not in reality?

We have wandered about the country, talking about Hawken rifles, showing our slides to Hawken enthusiasts, examining and photographing Hawken rifles, and we are constantly amazed at the infinite number of variations to be found in these guns. No two have appeared identical in every respect; with variants ap-

PLATE NO. 136

"Buffalo Hunt," an oil painting by Charles Russell, at Thomas Gilcrease Institute, Tulsa, Oklahoma.

pearing in every conceivable detail. Quality of workmanship also shows considerable fluctuation, reflecting the maker's skill, and perhaps the amount of workmanship the public would support. Hard times were often reflected in the cheaply made guns that, somehow surviving, have misled a few into believing all Hawken guns to be crude, and poorly made.

For instance, we submit that Samuel Hawken was appalled to come back from Denver and discover the quality of rifles that were being produced and stamped Hawken, St. Louis. His indignation is apparent, when one examines those rifles that reflect the above characteristics, and have the name Hawken obliterated by repeated overstamping with the St. Louis stamp. Dr. Veit, of Alton, Illinois, has such a rifle, and another one is in a private collection in southern Illinois. These rifles indicate that their quality, undeniable to lesser

degree than is common, was deemed by Samuel Hawken as not being worthy of the Hawken stamp. Another reason to believe it was necessary for Watt and Gemmer to purchase, in 1862, the right to use Sam's name. Certainly, the quality of workmanship improved after that date. The writer's personal opinion is that Gemmer went on to become an even better craftsman than either Jake or Sam.

We offer this volume with this admonishment. It is part of the Hawken story, and no more! Perhaps it embodies more information on the subject than any other publication heretofore offered, but it is not complete. It is only one small part, in a constantly growing drama. The more one learns, the more there seems to be of the thing, to be studied, mulled around, and applied against what has been said before. It gets kinda interesting, seems as though!

Index